YOU CAN'T LEAVE TILL YOU DO THE PAPERWORK: MATTERS OF LIFE AND DEATH

You Can't Leave Till You Do the Paperwork: Matters of Life and Death

Marcia Camp

With Contributions by
Clarissa Willis, Ph.D.

Copyright © 1999 by Marcia Camp.

Library of Congress Number:		99-91899
ISBN #:	Hardcover	0-7388-1356-7
	Softcover	0-7388-1357-5

Book's Subject or Genre: self-help, reference, grief, hospice, organ donation, last rites, patient's rights, child grief, unexpected death.

All rights reserved. No part of this book may be reproduced or transmitted in any form or by any means, electronic or mechanical, including photocopying, recording, or by any information storage and retrieval system, without permission in writing from the copyright owner.

This book was printed in the United States of America.

To order additional copies of this book, contact:
Xlibris Corporation
1-888-7-XLIBRIS
www.Xlibris.com
Orders@Xlibris.com

CONTENTS

What Others Are Saying About
  This Book 7
Introduction 9
Disclaimer 11

Chapter One
  Dealing with an Unexpected Death:
  Following the Paper Trail 13
Chapter Two
  Insurance, Wills and Trusts:
  Providing for Those Left Behind 23
Chapter Three
  Living Wills and Patient's Rights:
  Maximum Treatment Isn't Always Maximal Care 35
Chapter Four
  Hospice Home Care:
  A Concept About Living, Not Dying 43
Chapter Five
  Organ Donation:
  A Second Chance at Life 51
Chapter Six
  Planning Today's Funeral:
  How We Say Good-bye 63
Chapter Seven
  Cremation: Leaving the Land for the Living 73
Chapter Eight
  Cemeteries, Mausoleums, and Columbaria:
  Down to Earth or Heart-Level 81

Chapter Nine
  Bereavement, Grief, and the State of Mourning:
  Easing the Pain 89
Chapter Ten
  Helping the Young with Grief:
  Suffer the Little Children 107

Appendix 127
Index 202

What Others Are Saying About This Book

This is an excellent book that gives the reader a reliable, yet sensitive, resource to help understand many of the issues and emotions that people must face when a loved one dies. Simple, objective resources on such emotional topics are hard to find and certainly would be useful both to the general public and to public libraries.

Bobby Roberts, Ph.D.
Library Journal's 1997 Librarian of the Year

All of us are terminal— or mortal. All of us need to work through end-of-life issues. Ms. Camp's book is a great resource to help us on this journey. This book is a great help for pastors and caregivers.

The Reverend Doctor Karen K. Akin
Presbyterian Minister

Marcia Camp has provided us with a much needed, extremely important and comprehensive resource guide. It is extraordinarily well researched, easy to read and reference, and written with the sharp insight and compassion we have come to expect from the author. As none of us will escape the need for this information, it is a "must have" book.

Dr. Patricia Ingram Millikin
Family Therapist and Mental Health Columnist

Death is a subject few willingly care to address, but this well-written book provides helpful information, not only for the pre-planning for arrangements but in providing advice on related subjects.

Charlotte Tillar Schexnayder
Publisher and Legislator, Retired

This book has been thoughtfully and carefully researched. The material will be useful to the population at large because it answers questions that are important to all of us, and these answers are not easy to find.

Harold Luneau
University Senior Research Associate, Retired

A wonderfully informative book. The chapter about organ donation is certainly well documented.

Michael Manley
Executive Director of ARORA, an organ recovery agency

This book is a gold mine of information. It should be in every Family Practitioner's office library.

Gary Harper, M.D.
Private Practice Family Medicine

INTRODUCTION

Across the nation, seminars sponsored by churches, financial planners, hospice organizations and grief recovery groups are attended by eager participants, though the information they find is fragmented. The author has gathered information together in the most complete book of its kind to date.

Beginning with a hypothetical situation, each chapter leads the reader through a brief history, then into today's practices and options. Appropriate organizations, agencies, self-help groups, and recommended reading are liberally sprinkled throughout the book. Examples and quotations along with interesting and unusual approaches lighten the subject matter. This book provides much needed facts with sensitivity, humor, and insight.

The Appendix contains lists of names and addresses of agencies by state, and the Index lists particular subjects and terms for easy location. While each chapter is self contained and deals with one primary concern so that the book may be used as a reference, the reader would benefit from reading the book in its entirety. Many optimal choices are no longer an option at the time of need.

Disclaimer

This book does not endorse or promote any particular choice; it is intended only as an offering of practical options. General statements are made concerning acceptance of various practices by leading religions. It is assumed that each person/family will know the views and beliefs of their own religion or that they will consult clergy for clarification.

Agency and organization names, addresses, and phone numbers, as well as statistics, are the latest available to the author at press time. All these, as well as current laws, are constantly subject to change. Every effort has been made to compile information that is as complete and accurate as possible.

The book's purpose is to concisely inform the reader of important options, so that he/she may further investigate their suitability. The author and publisher are not engaged in rendering legal or other professional advice. Options selected should be further clarified by consulting qualified professionals. The author and publisher cannot be held responsible for losses incurred as a result of planning decisions and choices made by the reader.

Chapter One

Dealing with an Unexpected Death: Following the Paper Trail

The call came at 10 P.M., just as Chad was settling into his easy chair for the evening news. He was told to come to City Hospital—there had been a four-car pile-up on the freeway, and he was listed as the person to notify in case of emergency. One of the fatalities was Bob, his best friend since third grade. As he drove through a blur of traffic, he passed the field where they'd played Little League ball, past the church where he'd been best man in Bob's wedding—a marriage that ended in divorce. Chad hadn't even realized he was the person Bob listed on important papers, but then who else would he choose? The next trip across town, Chad would have Bob's best suit in the seat beside him, and he'd be initiated into a rite of passage few manage to avoid—making final arrangements for someone he loved.

Following the paper trail

Chad, like so many people approaching middle age, is "death innocent." He has never been near a dying person, never attended a funeral. The only thing he knows about circumstances surrounding these realities is what he's seen in the movies and on television. Whatever his preconceptions, reality is going to be quite different—not so much because it is sad and traumatic, but because death in the modern world is complicated by endless details. Someone has said, "you can't leave till all the paper work is done."

In the case of any unexpected death, the place to start is the address book. It should yield names, addresses, and phone numbers of family and close friends for immediate notification. An incredible amount of information must be uncovered in the first 24 - 36 hours after a death has occurred, usually a time of great emotional upheaval for survivors. Much of that information will be needed to plan last rites and write an obituary.

Obituaries

Obituaries have changed over time. They are seldom sentimental memorials of a person's life, they tend to carry just the facts. Most newspapers will publish a minimal death notice at no charge, then charge by the word for including additional information (funeral home personnel will help in preparing this).

Needed are age, place of birth, parents' names, and names of immediate family members (usually only spouse, children and grandchildren). Optional facts include colleges attended and degrees received; occupation/profession; honors received; military service; social and professional organizations; and if charitable contributions are suggested in lieu of flowers, end with the name of the charity or organization selected. Newspapers have varying policies concerning publication of photographs.

Among the first decisions to be made are arrangements for the funeral, burial, or cremation, which are discussed in Chapters Six and Seven. This must be settled even before the obituary can be completed, unless a second notice follows with details about time and place of last rites.

After contacting the next of kin, the person's employer and close co-workers should be notified. Organizations in which he/she carried responsibilities should be informed in case pending projects need to be shifted to other members, and, of course, friends and neighbors need to be told. If the person was prominent in the community, the press should be notified. Some newspapers have a featured obituary which includes interviews with friends and associates. Remember to inform hometown newspapers or publications in places important in that person's life.

Record-keeping

A system of record-keeping needs to be established early on for taking phone messages of condolence, as well as keeping up with expressions of sympathy whether in the form of visits, food, or flower arrangements. Someone needs to take charge of arrival and housing of out-of-town family members.

The funeral home will collect cards from flower arrangements, each of which will carry the giver's name, address, and a description of the arrangement. There will be thank-you notes furnished to the family by the funeral home, along with books signed during visitation and the final services.

The funeral home will secure the death certificate. Order at least a dozen if the deceased had a substantial amount of property, bank accounts, and other financial holdings (additional death certificates may be purchased later if needed). They are required by each insurance company, bank, and investment house where accounts are to be closed or transferred in case of joint ownership.

The search continues

If the survivors are dealing with meticulously kept records, their search for information will be easier, but this kind of discovery is never easy. In a perfect world, the following information would be readily at hand:

- Full legal name and Social Security number
- Health, home, life, and car insurance policy numbers with insurance company name and address
- Credit card account numbers and outstanding loan accounts listed with originating institutions and addresses
- Birth certificate
- Deeds and titles to property owned
- Marriage license(s) and divorce decree(s) if applicable
- Names and addresses of spouse and children (or death certificates of same)
- Copy of will or trust or location of same
- List of employer(s) and dates of employment
- Proof of citizenship, military service, and discharge
- Tax returns for three most recent years
- Safe deposit box location and key
- Membership in organizations, awards received
- Colleges attended and degrees received
- Preferences or pre-arrangements for funeral, cremation, burial and/or memorial service

If some of the above are not in evidence, the search intensifies. After the address book is exhausted, and hopefully the names of lawyer and accountant or financial advisor will be found there, the check registry, canceled checks, and deposit slips are of great importance. They will reveal financial obligations that need prompt attention, such as monthly payments that must be made. They will also identify regular sources of income. The landlord should be among the first to be notified.

If there is immediate need for money to keep a household operating, insurance policies are of prime interest, largely because they pay off quickly. The beneficiary only needs to notify the company and include a death certificate along with the policy number, or in some cases, the policy itself.

Locating all the insurance

Finding the major policies that have been paid on regularly throughout a lifetime may be the simplest part of the search. These are considered important papers and are usually found in lock boxes or other traditionally "safe" places. There may be other insurance coverage of which the insured was only vaguely aware. Survivors should:

- Notify the credit card companies. If the person died while traveling and made charges on those cards, there may be accidental death coverage.
- Call or write the personnel office of past and current employers and inquire about insurance coverage carried by the company and about possible death benefits.
- Find paycheck stubs which may also mention insurance, either health, hospital, or life.
- Check with insurance companies that carry the deceased's auto, home, or rental insurance. There may be small amounts of life insurance as part of those policies.
- Investigate loans whose payments may have built-in life insurance designed to retire the loan balances in the event of death.
- Look into organization memberships and correspond with major organizations (VFW, American Legion, business and professional organizations and unions) in which dues may include group life insurance.
- Read income tax returns. Some insurance policies pay

dividends, and these dividends will be declared as income on the return, thus alerting survivors of a policy in force.
- Check safe deposit boxes, if jointly held.
- Remember, warranties are a form of insurance. They may be found in or near the product under warranty.

Continue to look

Sleuthing doesn't stop with the usual places where important papers are kept. Desk drawers, at home and at work, are obvious places where papers are kept, but what about bureau drawers, chests, and trunks? Depending on the age and personality of the deceased, as well as their personal level of security, papers and money may turn up in odd locations.

An elderly woman stuffed large sums of cash in her gloves, thinking the housekeeper wouldn't think to look there if she rifled her chest of drawers. An octogenarian kept $300 in cash, along with car title and insurance papers, under the carpet of his car's trunk. He'd gotten a speeding ticket once in a strange town where checks weren't accepted, and he was forever after prepared for the worst. Don't forget health club lockers, glove compartments, and that portable file, the wallet.

The surviving spouse

Besides the sadness and trauma of loss and the flood of immediate (and permanent) decisions which must be made, each day in the return to normalcy brings a host of new questions and decisions.

The steps involved in carrying out directives of a will or trust are dealt with in Chapter Two, however, it is the everyday judgements that must be addressed right away. Of primary importance is family medical insurance. If it was obtained through the deceased's employment, spouse and dependent children may be able to continue in the employer's group plan. Under a federal law called COBRA, survivors may be entitled to continue under a spouse's work-related medical plan for up to 36 months by regularly paying premiums.

Check with most recent and former employers to see if health, accident, or life insurance with them will yield payments. The deceased may also be due a final paycheck for vacation or sick leave pay. Conversely, any Social Security check received after the person's death must be returned. If the death was work-related, there may be Workman's Compensation benefits. There may also be payments from pension plans or stock options.

Credit cards may have been issued to married couples in both names, but if issued only in the deceased person's name, timely payments should be made in order to protect the survivor's good credit. If the survivor has not established his or her own credit rating, they may experience difficulties in getting a new card. If this is the case, remember sometimes the local bank is the best place to get a credit card without having to put down a large deposit.

The bank and the IRS

In the case of **jointly held bank accounts** and **Certificates of Deposit** (CDs), all that is required is a visit to the bank with an original of the death certificate in hand to automatically transfer the account or CD to the survivor (no penalty or charge for early withdrawal will be assessed). In many cases, the bank official will photocopy the death certificate for his files and return the original to the joint owner, but banks will not accept a photocopy. It is a good idea to leave a checking account unchanged for a few weeks in the event that outstanding checks made payable to the deceased need to be deposited with "for deposit only" in lieu of an endorsement.

If the **safe deposit box** includes a joint signer, rights to the box pass immediately to the surviving account holder. If the box was in the deceased's name only, in most states a court order will be required to open the box, and then only the will and materials pertaining to death may be removed until such time as the will is probated.

Federal and state income taxes of the deceased are due for the year of death on the usual filing date the next year. A surviving spouse may file jointly for the year of death and for two additional years if there are dependent children.

Changes in ownership

Changes in ownership and title entail changes in legal responsibility. A joint owner or person with right of survivorship needs to be chosen at the time the new owner receives the account or property to ensure an equally smooth transition at the new owner's death. This is also true in the case of selecting new beneficiaries for the survivor's insurance policies. A new will should also be made by the survivor.

Concerning **jointly owned property** and **jointly incurred debt**, all bills should be forwarded to the personal representative or executor who is settling the estate, either as executor of the will or as trust officer (see Chapter Two). Every effort should be made to pay these debts promptly (mortgage payments, car payments, and utility bills) in order that the survivor may keep a good credit rating.

Legal issues

Use the services of a lawyer (one familiar with the deceased's business) or accountant (one familiar with his finances) in case there was an overall plan in effect to protect money and property from excessive taxation in the event of death.

These are some of the legal and financial details to be faced at the time of death of a family member or friend, yet there are personal emotional needs to be addressed too. Grief and the means to alleviate it are discussed in Chapters Nine and Ten.

Few people are willing to invest the time and effort to collect the information listed at the beginning of "The Paper Trail." It is a daunting task that seems unimportant except in contemplation of death and, even then, it is easier to leave undone. Be assured, someone will have to find all of it. At least prepare a "map" to the location of important papers, i.e., bank accounts, credit cards, and current obligations—right-hand desk drawer; deeds—bank safe deposit box; projects in progress for charitable/professional organizations—boxes in bedroom closet; (lawyer)has will; (accountant) knows investments and estate planning; final arrangements in fireproof file in den closet. This type directive can be handwritten on one page without leaving your easy chair.

All we're really doing is trying to make things easier for those who have to clean up and turn off the lights.
—*Bill Woodell, retired insurance executive*

Chapter Two

Insurance, Wills and Trusts: Providing for Those Left Behind

Henry is responsible, dependable, and conservative. He and his wife of 50 years worked hard, raised a family, acquired a little property, and saved for their old age. Somehow on the way to their golden years, the world became complex. The neighborhood, where their small house nestles on a 50 by 150 foot lot, has become the "in" place to live, and the property has appreciated beyond belief. Henry and Ruth have started drifting from one seminar to another, each outlining a labyrinth of estate tax laws and inheritance advice. None of the speakers is aware of the needs of the couple's children. One son has already borrowed his inheritance, another is involved in a messy divorce, and a third has ample income and security. Like many couples, they must wade through confusing information to arrive at unique personal decisions—decisions which are doomed if they fail to know all their options.

Distributing possessions

Henry and Ruth have come to that time in life when their thoughts are often about how their worldly possessions will be distributed. Whether it's the rural acreage where father and son hunted together or a treasured piece of furniture or heirloom jewelry, a verbal, "I'd like this to go to_____," leaves too much to chance.

From simple keepsakes to untold riches, where there's a will, there's a way to transfer ownership to the intended loved ones. A will can be as elementary as its owner wishes or as complex as the magnitude of the estate requires. Only about half the states recognize a simple, handwritten will, so if much property is at stake, it is best not to attempt a do-it-yourself will. Before consulting an attorney it is well to become familiar with a few terms and alternatives.

A will is the cornerstone

A **will** is the cornerstone of estate planning, and although the word **estate** has a lofty sound, it is simply all that you own plus all that is owed to you, minus that which you owe. At the time of death, that estate takes on a life of its own. It becomes a legal entity that will be distributed according to the laws of the state of residence. Unless plans have been made and appropriate actions taken, it may not go to those heirs who have been selected.

To be valid a will must be witnessed in accordance with state law. Many states require at least two persons not named in the will to be present when the will is signed. Be sure to sign or initial each page. A will is a legal document that transfers **assets** to heirs as the result of a death. The will often names the personal representative or **executor** who is responsible for making sure those assets, if they are complex or extensive, get to the correct **beneficiaries**, those people—spouse, children, friends, organizations or charities—who will benefit from the estate. A will describes the property and specifies the amount or share that passes to each beneficiary.

Only **probate property** is affected by a will, that is property subject to the probate court's oversight. When a person dies without a will (such a person is said to have died **intestate**) the court allots probate property according to a formula set by state law.

Warren Burger, Chief Justice of the Supreme Court longer than any other this century, prepared a woefully inadequate will. He typed a one-page will which failed to grant his executors the power to sell his real estate. The omission required a probate court's permission to sell property. Burger's $1.8 million estate was faced with federal and state taxes which he could have avoided.

Understanding probate

The word **probate**, comes from the Latin word meaning to prove. A will presented to probate court must have its validity proven. If it was not properly prepared or witnessed, the judge can ignore the will's instructions. Probate's other steps are: (1) to confirm the personal representative named in the will or appoint an executor if there is no will; (2) to inform creditors and beneficiaries that probate has started; (3) to inventory and appraise property; (4) to pay creditors, taxes, and fees; (5) to distribute property to beneficiaries and close the estate.

Probate is unnecessary if the decedent owned only **non-probate property**, i.e., jointly owned property, which passes by law to the surviving co-owner(s); life insurance and pension benefits and property owned in trust. Non-probate property passes to survivors outside the probate process and outside the terms of the will.

Property subject to probate generally includes (1) property that is owned (titled) in one person's name alone; (2) property owned jointly without a right of survivorship (as **tenants in common**); (3) life insurance paid to the person's estate (not directly to a person or organization); and (4) in community property states a spouse's share of the community or marital property. Such property is subject to the probate court's oversight whether or not the person who died left a will.

The problem with wills is not how much they cost to write but how much they cost to probate. Those costs include filing fees, property appraisal fees, bonding costs, and fees for attorneys. Attorneys may charge an hourly rate or a percentage of the estate's value. Shop around. Obviously a small or uncomplicated estate would best be handled at an hourly rate. Even so, the fees for will, probate, and attorney can be significant, even for a small estate.

Sometimes, a person's estate is small enough to qualify for **expedited probate** or other simple transfer procedures. Inquire at the probate court in your state to see if your estate might qualify. Limits in some states are relatively low, in others as much as $60,000.

Some people choose to avoid probate by owning property, bank accounts and Certificates of Deposit (CDs) jointly. In the case of **joint tenants** (co-owners with a right to survivorship), when one owner dies, the property passes immediately to the other(s). Although this looks worry-free, there can be problems. In the instance of bank accounts and CDs, the co-owner(s) can, at any time, withdraw the money or cash in the CDs. The bank accounts and CDs would also be exposed to claims of creditors of the other owner(s). A safer way of leaving money and property may be a living trust.

Revocable living trust

The **revocable living trust**, like the will, is a document that allows a person to leave property to family and others. Like a will, a living trust lets you choose the person who will divide your property according to your wishes, but unlike property that is willed, property placed in a living trust avoids probate.

The person who creates a trust is called a **settlor** or **grantor** and he names a **trustee** to manage the property according to terms of the trust. The settlor usually serves as the trustee, keeping control of the property to the end of his life, unless illness or accident incapacitates him. A revocable living trust allows the **successor trustee** to handle the settlor's financial affairs, such as signing checks and paying bills. A living trust makes guardianship or conservatorship unnecessary.

As the name implies, the settlor can change or completely revoke the trust, however when the settlor dies, the trust's terms cannot be changed. The successor trustee must follow the instructions of the trust and, after paying bills and death taxes, see that beneficiaries get their property. The settlor creates the trust by transferring property into the name of the trust—a trust does no good until you fund it, i.e., go to the bank and change the name on checking and savings accounts and CDs to the name of the trust. Visit the county Registrar of Deeds to change the title of home and other real property, and call your broker and change the name on stock certificates.

Pour-over will

If a living trust is executed, it is well to write a **pour-over will**, which passes to the trust any property that was not placed in trust. Living trusts are valid in all states and can direct the transfer of out-of-state property to beneficiaries anywhere and help avoid the expense of probate proceedings in multiple states. Avoiding probate ensures the speedy and private transfer of property.

Keep in mind that, as of January 1, 1998, the estate tax exemption on estates that include a family farm or business increased to $1.3 million if the heirs continue to run the enterprise. Estates that do not include a family farm or business had an exemption threshold of $625,000 in 1998, with gradual increases in the exemption up to $1 million by 2006.

While living, a person may transfer up to $10,000 to each person he chooses, each year free of gift taxes, and the amount is not counted against the $625,000 exemption. This money may also be given in the form of either educational (tuition) or medical expenses, provided payment is made directly to the educational institution or provider of medical care.

Buying insurance

Buying insurance is an affair of the heart for both young and old. There is a genuine need to take the emotion out of choosing insurance coverage, another means of providing for loved ones. Individual needs vary widely due to age, income, size of estate, debts, number and nature of heirs, financial situations, and the constant shifting of all these factors.

For young families, life insurance offers protection against premature loss of the breadwinner. Men used to be the only family member with insurance, but increasingly women feel the need to be insured because loss of their income would also impact the family's financial well-being.

Sometimes a persistent salesman takes advantage of a head-of-household's conscientiousness about providing for his/her family. He may then over-burden the young family's income with insurance premiums beyond its means. This can be as crippling to the family's financial security as being under-insured.

Older people with a stable income for the surviving spouse and little or no debt sometimes feel an overwhelming need for the sense of security that insurance affords. They want to go on providing after death and plan for benefits to pay debts incurred by a possible final illness and funeral expenses. This "traditional" head-of-house must be especially cautious because the potential for an insurance scam increases with the age of the insured. A *realistic evaluation of need* is the key.

Types of insurance

During a person's working life, he may be covered by **group life**, which offers lower rates because he is part of a large pool of people with favorable risk factors. But the selection process for people buying insurance on an individual-need basis can be formidable.

The life insurance business is a predictable one based on years of analysis of mortality rates. **Premiums** (monthly, quarterly, or yearly payments) are determined by the insured persons age, sex, and health. Sometimes even occupation, personal habits, and the area in which the insured lives are factored in.

All insurance plans or **policies** differ, but it may help to understand the three main categories before tailoring one of them to fit your unique needs. **Term life** insurance is usually the least expensive. It is purely for protection, providing only death benefits, with no savings element. Although it may be the best answer for immediate protection for a young person unable to afford more comprehensive types of insurance, the death benefit amount often decreases as the policy holder gets older. Term premiums climb rapidly and dramatically for older persons and often price themselves out of consideration for the wise consumer.

Ordinary life insurance, also called straight or whole life, has higher premiums, but the death benefit stays the same or increases with time. After the tenth year, policy dividends can sometimes be applied to the premium, in some cases equaling or surpassing the premium and creating a "vanishing premium" and a small amount of interest income in later years.

Many ordinary life policies also have **cash value** (the savings portion of the policy) which, after a set number of years, may be borrowed. In most cases, the borrowed amount will be deducted from the death benefit rather than paid back to the insurance company.

Universal life insurance, a product created in the 1970s, is an investment vehicle. It offers flexible premiums, flexible cash value, and a flexible death benefit, which can be raised or lowered within the policy's limits. Premiums are paid for ten, twenty, or thirty years, and policies are generally in effect for thirty years. Universal life policies seldom offer dividends, instead larger cash value accrues due to addition of interest income which fluctuates with the market. Higher premiums afford the insured an enforced investment which grows, as well as insurance coverage that assures a death benefit.

Shop around

With such a menu of choices, "shop around" is the name of the game. Start with an agent you trust and don't be put off by the daunting tables of figures. They can help you make a logical comparison if you choose to become involved in the decision-making process. One rule-of-thumb test for whether a policy may be a rip-off is: your premiums plus 5% interest should be less than the death benefits for the first ten years, otherwise, you'd be better off putting your money in a savings account.

Before a final decision, check the stability of the company in *Bests' Insurance Reports* at your local library. Note: When the original insurance company has changed ownership and cannot be located, call the State Insurance Commission for an up-dated name and address. (See Appendix for addresses by state).

Viatical settlements

Viatical settlements involve collecting life insurance benefits before death occurs. Collecting your own death benefits could help stave off excessive money worries during a terminal illness. Since 1988 when the first company began, over 60 viatical settlement companies have sprung up across the nation. They act as brokers for life insurance policy-holders whose terminal illnesses put them desperately in need of money at a time when they are helpless to earn any.

The term "viatical" comes from the Latin-based *viaticum* a word used for the Eucharist when administered to a person near death, and, earlier during the Roman Empire, it meant money and supplies given to officials before a risky journey.

While some see the new twist in insurance pay-offs as a ghoulish business fed by the insured's early death, others, primarily AIDS and cancer patients, see it as a way to maintain independence, keep their homes, and pay for needed medical treatment.

The investor-driven "death futures" which now amount to a

$350 million industry climbing at the rate of 25% each year, works like this. A viatical brokerage firm purchases the life insurance policy from a terminally ill person, known as the **viator**. Using money put up by investors, the brokerage firm then owns the policy, pays premiums and collects when the viator dies.

When the practice began, the policyholder only received about 60 cents on the dollar, but now, depending on the attractiveness of their policies, viators can command 70% to 80% of the policy's death benefit.

Once benefits have been signed over to the investment group, routine inquiries, usually monthly, are made about the health of the viator (usually through his/her physician, friend, or family member). At the insured's death, the company, as policy owner, collects the benefits.

Those contemplating this early insurance pay-off should be aware that there may be tax implications and the possible loss of public assistance benefits. A list of viatical companies may be obtained by calling/writing either of the two non-profit organizations listed below:

Viatical Association of America
1200 Nineteenth Street, N.W.
Washington, D.C. 20036-2412
(202) 429-5113
(http://www.viatical.org)

National Viatical Association
1030 Fifteenth Street, N.W.
Washington, D.C. 20005
(800) 741-9465
(http://www.nationalviatical.org)

The overlooked life insurance

And then there's that old stand-by **Social Security**, an often overlooked form of life insurance. When we hear the words Social

Security, we think of retirement checks (and indeed over 43 million Americans receive retirement income from the government). But in a very real way, Social Security offers a broad kind of life insurance for workers' survivors. In many cases, it is more valuable than commercial life insurance.

For the average wage earner with a family, Social Security benefits are equal to a $300,000 life insurance policy or a $200,000 disability insurance policy.

When a person dies after working and paying into Social Security, survivor benefits can be paid to widows, widowers, children, dependent parents, and sometimes surviving divorced spouses. Although the deceased worker must have the required number of work credits to qualify for survivors' benefits, under a special rule, benefits can be paid to his/her children and the spouse caring for them even if the worker has credit for only one and a half years of work in the three years prior to his/her death. It is estimated that 98 out of every 100 children *could get benefits* when a working parent dies.

Eligibility for benefits

Those eligible for survivors benefits are:

- Widow or widower—full benefits at age 65 or older or reduced benefits as early as 60
- A disabled widow or widower may obtain benefits at 50 - 60
- Widow or widower at any age if he/she has care of deceased's child under 16 or disabled who gets benefits
- Unmarried children under age 18 (up to 19 if attending elementary or secondary school full time)
- Deceased worker's child qualifies for benefits at any age if disabled before age 22 and remains disabled
- Under special circumstances, benefits may be paid to

stepchildren or grandchildren
- Dependent parents 62 years of age or older
- Divorced, retirement-aged spouses whose marriage lasted at least 10 years

Divorced spouses

If the divorced spouse is eligible for one-half of worker's earned Social Security retirement, his/her monthly check increases to 80% of worker's monthly retirement benefit when he/she dies. This applies to any of the deceased worker's divorced spouses whose marriages lasted at least ten years, and the payment does not decrease the amount received by his/her widow/widower.

Typical situations

Although the deceased worker's benefit is based on lifetime earnings, percentage depends on recipient's age and benefit for which he/she is eligible. Below are typical situations:

- Widow or widower age 65 or older: 100%
- Widow or widower 60 - 64: about 71% - 94%
- Children: 75%

Generally, survivor's benefits cease upon remarriage, but remarriage after 60 (50 if disabled) will not prevent benefit payments. Remarriage at 62 or older may make the survivor eligible for benefits on the record of the new spouse if those benefits are higher.

Information needed for benefits

Certain information and documents are necessary for survivors to receive benefits. They include:

- Your Social Security number and that of deceased worker

- Your birth certificate
- Your marriage certificate if you are a widow, widower, or divorcee
- Your divorce papers if applying as divorced spouse of at least ten years
- Children's birth certificates
- Deceased worker's W-2 forms or Federal Self-Employment forms
- Tax return for most recent year
- Death certificate
- Checkbook or savings passbook if you want checks direct deposited rather than sent through the mail

There is a special one-time death-benefit payment of $255 that can be made only to certain family members. For more information call 1-800-772-1213 between 7:00 AM and 7:00 PM or send for *Survivors* (Publication #05-10084) and *How Work Affects Social Security Benefits* (Publication #05-10069) by calling your local Social Security office or going on line at http://www.ssa.gov.

Chapter Three

Living Wills and Patient's Rights: Maximum Treatment Isn't Always Maximal Care

Miriam has been a career woman all her adult life. An only child, she knows the weight of making hard decisions and taking responsibility. Toward the end of his life, her father was in and out of hospital, often subjected to procedures Miriam deeply questioned. Now her mother's Alzheimer's disease has advanced to its final stages. Miriam became aware of the challenges and pitfalls of medical care for the terminally ill with her own parents, and she also witnessed the uncertainty and hopelessness of siblings conferring in hospital waiting rooms. She decided to take some responsibility off the shoulders of her own daughter, should she become unable to make decisions about her care. Miriam will put to good use the sensible legal options and choices which she has learned are available to her.

Planning in the technological age

Miriam is not only shielding her daughter from making tough decisions, she is also putting her own mind at ease. With the beginning of the hospice movement in the early 1970s and with Elizabeth Kubler-Ross's popularization of the spiritual aspects of death and dying, a new awareness of the dying process emerged. This awareness was further increased by the AIDS epidemic.

Too often, people were dying alone in the technological context of hospitals, often pharmaceutically diminished and separated from loved ones. Under those circumstances, death was justifiably feared.

Maximum treatment is not always maximal care, and individuals need to exert some control over medical decision making. Today there are legal means available to take some of the guesswork and chance out of the end of life. Taking positive steps toward making highly personal decisions need not be a time of sad and morose thoughts.

Living wills

Having a **living will** is one way people can limit the use of extraordinary measures to prolong life. These documents relieve individuals of a number of life's "what ifs," affording peace of mind for themselves and ultimately their families. Granted, it is everyone's privilege to demand aggressive treatment for himself or a loved one, to the extent that his resources will permit, and certainly today's laws favor that approach to health care delivery. This chapter is meant to clarify and familiarize the reader with various avenues available to avoid anxiety over the possibility of being sustained in a vegetative state for a long period of time. Most of these efforts can be put into motion early in life, even though each is directed primarily at life's end.

A living will is an **advance directive** or **health care declaration**—a legal document which informs your physician(s) about the medical treatment you do and do not want if you have a terminal condition, especially if you cannot communicate your wishes.

Some of the treatments usually included in a living will are artificial feeding, artificial breathing, surgery, drugs, and cardiopulmonary resuscitation (CPR). A person may write in any other specific instructions desired. The directive can include care during a persistent vegetative state, which is not necessarily a terminal case within the meaning of the law. Living wills do not allow withdrawal of comfort measures such as pain medication, in fact, the will can demand that adequate pain relief be given. Because they become operational only when the patient is terminally ill, a living will can be revoked by the signer at any time.

Patient Self-Determination Act

Since the **Patient Self-Determination Act** became law in 1991, every patient over the age of 18, when admitted to a hospital, must be given the opportunity to declare an advance directive.

The hospital must by law (1) provide the patient with written information about his rights under state law to accept or reject treatment; (2) inform him about his right to name a person who will have **durable power of attorney** and be his surrogate decision-maker should he be unable to make decisions for himself; (3) document in his medical records whether or not he has an advance directive; and (4) provide the same treatment options whether or not he has such a directive. The hospital cannot require the patient to sign a living will, however, the hospital is required to inform him of his right to have one. Neither is he required to name a proxy. The patient's response to these documents becomes part of his medical records.

The occasion of entering a hospital is a less than optimal time to be introduced to such information. All advance directives are not the same. Some offer a plethora of options and combinations of choices that need thorough examination and contemplation. A living will form may be obtained by calling Choice in Dying at 1-800-989-WILL or you may compose your own.

Keep your directive current

Clarifying your general wishes and philosophies regarding life, death, and medical care may be better than trying to pinpoint specific treatments and procedures under particular conditions. Remember that treatments change, technology advances, and cures are found, so keep your directive current. Your views and wishes may change, and you have the right to revoke or alter your advance directive at any time. This document is valid for anyone over the age of 18 when signed and witnessed by two people other than family members.

It is important to let the family know your wishes and where they can locate your executed living will, should it become necessary—don't keep it in a safe deposit box. Discuss the subject with your physician when you give him/her a copy of the document, and if he cannot in good conscience agree with your directives, you may want to find a doctor who can.

No judgement of malpractice has ever been handed down against a doctor for following the terms of a living will or a rational patient's instruction to withhold care. Some courts have convicted doctors of assault and battery for providing treatments against patients' wishes.

In a recent study published in the *Journal of the American Medical Association* (JAMA), advance directives were not available 74% of the time, thus were not honored. Yet when medical providers were aware of the patient's directive, it influenced treatment in 86% of cases. It was noted that nursing homes often failed to send a copy of the directive with other medical information when a patient was transferred to the hospital.

Healthcare proxy

This brings up the subject of a **healthcare proxy**, a person who will make needed decisions if the patient cannot. Without a proxy, and in the absence of a living will, the patient's next of kin will be asked to decide further medical care issues, and in the case of the presence of several relatives of equal responsibility (such as adult children), this could create problems.

A properly drafted **healthcare power of attorney** goes much further by naming a person to make any health-care decision for him if the person in question is unable to make such decisions for himself. This document also states the individual's health care preferences, and the agent must act in accordance.

End-of-life choices are controversial

In some states, a living will does not guarantee that an individual's desire not to be kept alive by life-sustaining treatment will be honored. When a person moves from one state to another, he should check laws in the new place of residence. At this writing, there is no uniformity in laws of this nature. The living will is merely a directive to the physician(s) to withhold or withdraw such procedures in case of terminal illness. For further information, order Health Care Powers of Attorney, Order #D-13895 from:

AARP Fulfillment EE0372
P. O. Box 22796
Long Beach, CA 90801-5796
http://www.aarp.org

Because the subject of end-of-life choices is a controversial one with some institutions and in some geographical areas, there have been instances in which doctors and/or hospital have refused to honor a patient's advance directive. This places the matter in the province of the courts.

Elder law

In the event that a hospital attempts to force treatment, a lawyer specializing in elder law may be consulted. He will advise the hospital's legal staff of the consequences of refusing to honor the patient's advance directive. The attorney may have to obtain a court order directing the doctor to withhold medical treatment. Elder law referrals are available through http://www.seniorlaw.com or by writing:

The National Academy of Elder Law Attorneys
655 N. Alvernon Way, Suite 108
Tucson, AZ 85711

Without living will or health proxy

If a person has neither living will nor health proxy, decisions are usually made with consensus of the family and the patient's doctor(s). That leaves decisions up to individuals whose motives and values may conflict with those of the patient. Doctors bring their own personal and professional ethics into the discussion, and governing all these are hospital policy and state and federal laws. In controversial cases, the courts may be called upon to make the final call, and this can take months or years, adding to the turmoil, heartache, and overwhelming costs to often distraught family members.

In some states, living wills are only valid for the **terminally ill** who are faced with imminent death, and they may not include people who are **permanently unconscious.** Sometimes they include only those who are expected to live a few days or hours. One state's law defines a terminal condition as "an incurable and irreversible condition that, without the administration of life-sustaining treatment, will . . . result in death within a relatively short time." Another state's requirement says that death would result in six months "with or without the intervention of treatment."

While physicians in the 1970s were against living wills, the climate has changed dramatically. Since the enactment of the Patient Self Determination Act, attitudes have changed. Also, in 1991, Derek Humphry's *Final Exit*, which contained detailed information about euthanasia as a form of self-deliverance, remained for months at the top of the New York Times Best Seller List.

In 1995, Sherwin Nuland's *How We Die*, a compassionate but starkly revealing look at the ways life ends, rose to the top tier of best seller lists. The success of both these books shows that people are becoming more interested in their own death and making decisions concerning how it comes to pass.

Interest in living wills has soared since former President Richard Nixon and former First Lady Jacqueline Kennedy Onassis used their living wills to avoid use of heroic efforts to prolong their lives. Nuland's words could become the credo for those who wish to make informed choices, "I will not die later than I should simply for the senseless reason that a highly skilled technological physician does not understand who I am."

Any competent adult has the right to refuse medical treatment, medicine, and orders to go to or stay in a hospital. Contrary to popular belief, a person has the common law right to refuse treatment and walk out of a hospital against doctor's orders, though he will be asked to sign a form agreeing not to sue the doctor or the hospital if his condition worsens.

Maria Rodriguez, a nurse in Gary, Indiana, had a living will tattooed on her stomach featuring a red heart slashed with the universal "no" sign and the words "no code," followed by "Pain and comfort only. Organ donor."

Hospice care

Hospice care may be the answer when the decision is made to refuse unwanted treatment. A recent Gallup poll from the National Hospice Organization showed that nine out of ten Americans prefer to be cared for and die at home. The hospice concept, with its emphasis on palliative rather than curative care, allows terminally ill patients to live out the final months of life at home with as much comfort and dignity as possible.

Finally, the Supreme Court has ruled that artificially supplied feeding and hydration are medical treatments and therefore can be refused or withdrawn on a par with other medical treatment. The American Academy of Neurologists has stated that patients in a persistent vegetative state are incapable of experiencing pain, so ceasing to provide food and water cannot cause suffering. It is important for everyone to know his legal rights in the state in which he lives. To get information about your state's laws, contact:

Choice in Dying
325 East Oliver Street
Baltimore, MD 21202
(800)-989-9455
http://www.choices.org

Chapter Four

Hospice Home Care:
A Concept About Living, Not Dying

John is one of six children—a member of a large and happy family. When his mother was widowed at the age of 80, he was the logical one to take her into his empty nest, though he and his wife often give shelter to their children in transition between jobs and marriages. His brothers and sisters live out-of-state, and his mother would have been forced to leave her few remaining friends. Now John's mother has been diagnosed with cancer in its terminal stages. John and his wife Mary are in their early 60s, and they have medical problems of their own, but they want to care for his mother at home if at all possible. The hospital social worker tells them about help that sounds like a modern day miracle—something called hospice home care.

Hospice care

John is lucky. A scant 20 years ago, he would have probably had no option but to place his mother in the unfamiliar setting of a skilled care nursing home or hospital. Although surveys show that most people would rather die at home than in hospital, many are unaware of **hospice** service and how to benefit from this alternative care program.

The hospice concept, with its emphasis on palliative rather than curative care, allows terminally ill patients to live out the final months of life as comfortably as possible at home instead of in a hospital. They are able to carry on alert, pain-free lives and to manage symptoms of their diseases so that their remaining days can be spent in dignity and comfort. Hospice is about living, not dying.

The hospice movement, which offers specialized quality care for the terminally ill, arose in direct response to the frustration felt by consumers and health care professionals. They recognized that the current fragmented practices were not dealing adequately with the physical, psychological, and emotional needs of the terminally ill.

Historical perspective

In earlier times, when dying was done primarily at home, the family was naturally involved in providing care. Until the late 1800s, death was viewed as a natural process. By the mid-nineteen-seventies, more than 70% of deaths were occurring in hospitals or other institutional settings. Families were scattered from coast-to-coast, and care for the dying was almost solely in the hands of health care workers. Since dying at home was no longer an experience shared by family, a mystique arose about death itself, and it had become a subject not to be discussed.

As the practice of long-term hospitalization replaced at-home care, families became isolated from the patient both physically and emotionally. Dying patients were treated in the same manner and with the same methods used on patients who were expected to recover. This "medical model" of treatment had no provisions for dealing with the emotional, psychological, and spiritual needs of the patient who was never going to get well.

Today's concept of hospice began in England in 1967, when Dr. Cicely Saunders pioneered the first way-station for the terminally ill. The term "hospice" is derived from the same Latin root word as hospitality. Medieval hospices were resting places for sick or weary travelers. The hospice movement in the United States began in the mid-seventies as a result of society's changing attitudes about death. Although England focused on specialized hospitals where patients could receive the type of inpatient treatment they needed, the focus in America maintained the patient at home or in as home-like an environment as possible.

Comprehensive approach

The hospice model is a comprehensive approach to care with attention concentrated on both patient and family as a unit of care. The team approach is used in treatment. Physicians, nurses, social workers, counselors, clergy members, and volunteers all work together as equal partners in providing for the various needs of the patient-family unit.

While hospice began as a grass-roots organization with small groups of interested individuals, its philosophy has grown to encompass larger organizations such as hospitals and hospice agencies, both for-profit and non-profit.

A new wind seems to be blowing through our society . . . I speak of a new willingness to allow death to be an experience of profound spiritual dimension rather than an experience to be denied at all costs.
—The Right Reverend Larry E. Maze

Pain management

Very few physicians currently receive training in end-of-life palliative care, and many patients fail to benefit from the aggressive treatment of pain that is possible and recommended. Some doctors refuse to prescribe heavy doses of medication, fearing they will be criticized by society or that their patients will become addicted. For these reasons, the philosophy of hospice, geared entirely to physical and emotional comfort, is the humane choice for the terminally ill. It is the kind of alternative that, for many, can put some degree of quality in a patient's last days.

A terminally ill person needs the support of friends and family, a sense of transcendence, and doctors and nurses who make it clear that the patient will not be abandoned or left in pain. Florida, with its large elderly and AIDS populations, has nine of the nation's 15 largest hospices, including Boca Raton's Hospice-by-the-Sea, which serves 2,400 patients a year.

For hospice care in your area, check the Yellow Pages. For further information about all end-of-life care options, contact Compassion in Dying at 206-624-2775. Choice in Dying, a non-profit organization offers information about options including hospice and provides sample copies of living wills, phone 1-800-989-9455 (http://www.choices.org).

Solid support for distressed families

In 1997, the National Hospice Organization listed over 3,000 hospice agencies scattered through every state in the U.S. With its philosophy of enhancing life as long as life lasts, hospice provides a core inter-disciplinary team of professionals and volunteers who offer medical, psychological, and spiritual support for the terminally ill and assistance to their families.

Hospice treats the person instead of the disease, emphasizing the quality of life rather than its duration. It allows patients and families to experience the end of life together in the comfort and security of home or a home-like setting. Medicare-certified hospices are required to provide nursing care, social services, physician services, counseling services as well as home aide and homemaker services. Short-term inpatient care is provided for pain control and symptom management and for respite when necessary for the care giver. Continuous care in the home and medical equipment and supplies, including drugs, are available. Bereavement services are also offered.

Medicare and Medicaid

To be eligible under the Medicare Hospice Benefit, a person must be certified by a physician as having a terminal illness with a life expectancy of six months or less. Hospice is available to all terminally ill individuals and their families regardless of their age, gender, race, nationality, creed, sexual orientation, availability of a primary care giver, or ability to pay. Well over half of patients have conditions related to cancer, but other diagnoses include heart and lung disease, AIDS, and neurological disorders such as Alzheimer's disease and ALS. Hospice served over 540,000 patients and their families in 1998.

When provided by a Medicare-approved agency or organization, hospice care is covered almost 100% by Medicare Hospital Insurance (Part A). Most private insurance and managed care plans also pay for hospice care. There are also Medicaid programs in all 50 states, the District of Columbia, Guam, and Puerto Rico, and 80% of U.S. hospitals are Medicaid certified and can give hospice care. For more information about the Medicare program, order: "The Medicare Handbook" by calling 1-800-638-6833. Or write:

The National Hospice Organization
1901 N. Moore St., Suite 901
Arlington, VA 22209
800-658-8898
http://www.nho.org

Military personnel

Military personnel and their dependents can receive hospice care under the Civilian Health and Medical Program of the Uniformed Services (CHAMPUS). Veterans Affairs hospitals offer a hospice-type environment in certain wards, and families are encouraged to visit often and can receive counseling from a hospice team.

We fail to understand what patients with terminal disease ask of us. They are commonly too realistic to expect that we can take away the whole, hard thing that is happening. Instead they ask for concern and care for their distress and symptoms. Above all, they ask for our total awareness of them as people. At no time in the total care of the patient is this of greater importance.

—*Dr. Cicily Saunders*

Volunteers

Of the 115,000 persons involved in hospice care in America, some 95,000 are volunteers. Each year, they give more than five million hours to help dying persons and their families. Without them, most hospices would be unable to carry on their work.

Volunteers are the heart of hospice, and they provide assistance at all levels of skill. Many are friends or relatives of former hospice patients, and, having seen the positive affects of hospice, they want to continue its good work. Volunteers must undergo a rigorous training program before they can assist in patient care.

The number one response from hospice patients and families in a recent survey was "why didn't we know about hospice sooner?"

All too often, referrals are made to hospice at the very end of a terminal illness, and the hospice team is unable to address all the needs of the terminally ill and their families. Hospice services are available seven days a week, 24 hours a day. The nursing staff bears primary responsibility, and they call on other resources as necessary.

A personal alternative

But what about people dealing with a terminal illness who have not yet reached that final six months? There is another fledgling movement that is growing from this need for help at a very personal level.

The idea had its genesis in 1988, at a meeting of a dozen friends of a 42-year-old woman in the final stages of her life. The divorced mother of two girls in their late teens asked her friends to become the family she did not have nearby but desperately needed.

At that meeting, the woman explained that she would need help in every area of her life, caring for her children when she was hospitalized; helping to cook and clean while she recuperated from chemotherapy; getting her to appointments and so on.

In the next three and a half years, the group of friends started uncovering skills that people don't really think of as skills. Many had never been ill themselves and had no experience with a sick person. They quickly organized themselves into teams with two serving as captains to see that everything that needed doing got done. "Oh my gosh, what can *I* do?" quickly revealed what each person was good at, and they did it.

They called themselves the Funny Family, and soon they were handling insurance paperwork and organizing medication. As time passed, they shopped for a college wardrobe with the younger daughter and organized a wedding for the older one (with a wedding date set forward to accommodate her mother's flagging strength).

Their mutual friend died in 1991, and at her memorial service, one of the friends was asked, "Are you a national organization? Do you rent out?" It was then that they realized that what they had done needed to be perpetuated.

Funny Family members Cappy Capossela and Sheila Warnock wrote *Share the Care: How to Organize a Group to Care for Someone Who is Seriously Ill* (Fireside Books, a division of Simon & Schuster). As a result, groups have been formed in California, New Mexico, New York, Virginia, Colorado, Florida, Illinois, Nevada, and Wyoming. And caring for those who can't care for themselves got a boost from loving American ingenuity.

For more on this subject read *A Guide to Dying at Home* by Deborah Duda. A recommended resource is Daughters of the Elderly Bridging the Unknown Together (DEBUT)

Caregiver Resource Center
645 S. Rogers
Bloomington, IN 47401
Phone: (812) 339-1691

Chapter Five

Organ Donation: A Second Chance at Life

Corky recognizes her doctor's voice on the phone and wonders why he's calling. He isn't returning her call—she feels fine and he sounds grave. Then the carefully chosen words begin to take on meaning. He's trying to soften the blow, telling her that Eric, her husband of 25 years, has been struck by a passing motorist while on his afternoon bike ride—massive head injuries—she needs to get to the hospital immediately. Driving the route she developed when the boys were young, and trips to the emergency room were almost routine, she feels angry. This wasn't supposed to happen. With both kids away at college, she and Eric were finally going to have time for each other. Was it all about to be taken away? The words "next of kin" are about to take on a whole new meaning.

Second chance at life

Corky and her doctor have come together at the hospital emergency room under sad and stressful conditions. He has told her that Eric's accident has left him unable to recover, and, when life support is removed, he will die. The hospital is now required by federal law to discuss organ donation with Corky, a task he doesn't look forward to.

Organ and tissue donation affords a second chance at life, and Americans overwhelmingly support organ donation for transplantation. As early as 1993, a survey conducted by the Gallup Organization revealed that a majority would be willing to donate their organs upon death, and nearly all would honor the request of a family member who wished to become on organ donor.

So why has the number of donors remained almost unchanged over the past several years, annually hovering between 4,000 and 5,000 in spite of a growing success rate in transplantation and acceptance of the procedure as almost commonplace? For every transplant there must be donor, and organ procurement organizations work hard to educate the public so that they can make informed decisions well in advance of death.

Because technology made so many new life-saving procedures viable and the need for donors became acute, a young Tennessee senator named Al Gore sponsored federal legislation in 1987. The resulting Required Request Act mandates that hospitals discuss the options of organ and tissue donation with the family of any patient considered to be a potential donor.

Waiting lists

More than 60,000 Americans are on waiting lists for a kidney, heart, liver or other vital organs. One-third will die while waiting for an available organ. While thousands die under circumstances that would allow them to become donors, they become missed opportunities to give the gift of life.

According to the April, 1999, UNOS National Patient Waiting List for organ transplants, the following number of people are waiting for a transplant: kidney 41,117, liver 12,546, pancreas 449, pancreas islet cell 118, kidney-pancreas 1,819, intestine 117, heart 4,205, heart-lung 247, lung 3,200: total 61,999.

Transplant facts

- The number on waiting lists has increased 41% in the last two years, yet *donations have leveled off.*
- 18,000 lives were saved through transplants in 1996.
- An average of nine people die each day while waiting for a transplant.
- 40% of Americans consider organ transplantation experimental surgery. It is not.
- 85% of the population support organ donation yet each year 14,000 die who could be donors.
- Adding to the donor crisis is the fact that only 1,000 of the 6,000 acute care hospitals actually produce organs.

Types of death

Lack of understanding and numerous misconceptions stand in the way of greater participation. Perhaps the most fundamental information that needs clarification is just what conditions must occur for organ donation to take place. There are two kinds of death— **cardiac death** and **brain death**. The former is the type from which a person can be medically revived—theirs are the "coming back to life" stories. Over two million suffer cardiac death in the U.S. each year. Brain death is irreversible: there is no survival, and after a patient has been declared brain dead, life support, which merely keeps the heart pumping, *will be turned off* without the necessity for decisions by physician and/or family. It is the 20,000 to 25,000 who suffer brain death each year who could be organ donors.

To ease the trauma of family members having to decide on

organ donation in the midst of grief and adjustments that must be made in the hours just before or after a loved one's death, the thoughtful person will have made this decision.

Anyone 18 years of age or older can specify that he wishes to donate any or all organs or tissue such as corneas, heart valves, skin, bone, and bone marrow. There are state donor organizations, and drivers license bureaus provide space on an individual's drivers license to mark as a donor.

Louisiana is the only state in which drivers license applicants, on site at motor vehicle registry offices, are actively encouraged to sign and have witnessed a document for organ donation. This effort is in cooperation with Louisiana's donor registry whose information will in turn be entered into the state's hospitals' data banks to assure that donor's wishes will be carried out. As of 1997, five states offered organ procurement agencies access to their drivers licensing department records of potential donors name, address, birth date, and limitations on the purposes of the anatomical gift.

Many of the 1,500 to 2,000 Louisiana donors who register each month ask "can you guarantee that family members will not override my wishes?" Even when donor forms are properly executed and witnessed, the federal law of Required Consent prohibits donation if the legal next of kin objects. All organ retrieval agencies are watching the outcome of Louisiana's bold attempt to make the individual's wishes binding.

Between the time of Mickey Mantle's death in early August and late October, 1995, more than three million donor cards were distributed, each bearing the baseball legend's photo and batting statistics on the reverse side. Mantle, the recipient of a donor's liver, said, "I guess you could say I got another time at bat."

Misconception and mistrust

Misconception and mistrust combine to make organ donation a difficult decision for some individuals and families. Half of those surveyed do not believe organs are distributed fairly. However, in 1986, the federal government created by law the Organ Procurement and Transplantation Network (OPTN) to assure equal access for all patients needing organ transplants, regardless of circumstance. All U.S. transplant centers and organ procurement organizations are required to be members of OPTN.

Once hospital or organ procurement personnel have received consent for tissue or organ donation, the process is federally regulated and carried out with respect for the donor. After being declared brain dead (all activity above the brain stem has ceased), the donor organs are stabilized while an appropriate recipient is located and notified.

All organ procurement organizations are connected by computer to the United Network of Organ Sharing (UNOS), whose main computer is in Richmond, Virginia. A search is made for the person in greatest need of that particular organ or tissue based on criteria such as urgency of need, length of time on the waiting list, compatibility of blood type, tissue matching, and body size, all without regard to sex or race. Only after finding the best match are people's names and addresses considered in an effort to find a recipient. He or she is then notified and rushed into a hospital for transplant surgery.

Organ Donation By By Year	1988	1989	1990	1991	1992	1993	1994	1995	1996	1997
Kidney	5689	5712	6401	6661	6810	7460	7805	8293	8576	8669
Liver	1883	2374	2882	3187	3367	3799	4155	4368	4514	4639
Pancreas	582	803	953	1067	1007	1245	1363	1287	1310	1319
Heart	1792	1789	2179	2202	2247	2443	2529	2497	2476	2423
Lung	130	191	276	399	526	802	950	930	790	866

Removal and retrieval

In the case of a heart transplant, usually the same surgeon removes the organ and transplants it as well. In the case of other organs and tissue, skilled surgical teams remove and prepare the organs, which are kept chilled and transported to their destinations.

Organ retrieval is done by a transplant team under sterile conditions, and the donor's body is not disfigured. Tissue and organ donation will not delay funeral arrangements nor will it add to the cost of life-saving procedures. Organ donation is supported by all major religions.

> *"A— F— will not only get credit in heaven above for the four people alive, walking around with her organs, but the many hundreds who will be saved because other people will be inspired to follow her example."*
>
> —Rabbi Moshe D. Tendler
> Yeshiva University
> Authority on Jewish Medical Ethics

Billing stops with donation

Hospital billing to the donor's family stops before any of the recovery procedures begin. Every test that is made, every machine that is still in use as well as all surgical procedures connected with organ removal are billed to the organ procurement organization and eventually to the organ recipient. The National Transplant Act of 1984, prohibits the sale of organs, and the donor may not designate the recipient.

> *The first time ever that newspaper columnists Abigail Van Buren (Dear Abby) and Ann Landers wrote about the same subject on the same day, both made clarifications about a medical bill sent to a donor's mother in Florida.*

Confidentiality

The identity of the donor is kept confidential, though some organ recovery agencies allow correspondence through their agencies between donor families and recipients. If both parties agree to have contact, the agency will arrange it.

Surveys show that families almost always honor the wishes of a relative to donate organs and tissue. It is not only a humanitarian act, it is also the last request they can carry out for their loved ones. For more information about organ donation contact: The Coalition on Donation (888-TX-INFO1), National Donor Family Council of the National Kidney Foundation or http://www.organdonor.gov.

Success stories

In 1995, a California boy's parents were awarded Italy's highest civil decoration for donating their son Nicholas Green's organs to seven Italians after bandits killed the seven-year-old boy on an isolated highway in Italy.

. . . .

Five hours and 51 minutes after it stopped in Tennessee, Patti Szuber's heart was beating in her father's chest in Michigan. The unusual father-daughter operation ended Chester Szuber's four-year wait for a transplant after his youngest child was killed in a car accident. Patti had indicated a desire to donate her organs. Her liver and kidneys were given to other recipients.

. . . .

Timothy Heidler, 40, who lost his voice in a motorcycle accident 19 years earlier, rasped "Hi, Mom" at a Cleveland hospital just three days after he received a larynx transplant. The procedure was last performed in 1969 in Belgium, because of controversy in the medical community over risks vs. benefits of transplanting a non-vital organ.

Eye donation and corneal transplantation

Corneal transplants are the most frequently performed human transplant procedures. Forty-eight thousand corneal transplants were performed in the U.S. in 1998. Still there were more than 5,000 people on waiting lists throughout the country who were blind for no reason other than a shortage of available donor tissue. Over 90% of these operations successfully restore vision to persons suffering from corneal problems. Eye banks are non-profit organizations often associated with a hospital or university. They obtain and distribute donor eyes and, to ensure patient safety, they obtain the donor's medical history and evaluate it in accordance with the Eye Bank Association of America's (EBAA) strict Medical Standards.

Facts to consider

- Eye donation is a gift of sight to others and is consistent with beliefs and attitudes of major religions.
- Eye tissue procurement is performed within hours after death, so families may proceed with funeral arrangements.
- Great care is taken to preserve the donor's appearance, and no one will be able to tell that the procedure has been done.
- The gift of sight is made anonymously.
- Tell your family of your wishes, then complete the back of your drivers license.
- You may also obtain a donor card from your local eye bank or EBAA.

Anyone can be a donor—you do not need perfect vision to donate. Over one-quarter of donors in 1996 were over 70 years of age.

Body donation

Body donation is totally different from and has no association with organ and tissue donation. Bodies are needed by Departments of Anatomy of medical schools for both teaching and research. Because special embalming is required, it is advisable for donors to register with the department of a particular school and understand their specific needs in advance. It is also well to have consensus with family members because of the need for immediate notification of the institution following death.

With the increased demand for doctors, nurses, physical therapists, and other health service professionals, there is a growing need for anatomical subjects to be used to demonstrate and practice new surgical techniques. New programs in the field of physical therapy have also added to the demand. Research is the basis of all medical knowledge in the study of human anatomy. Without this study, there could be neither doctors nor surgery, alleviation of disease nor repair of physical injury. The practice of body donation is approved by Catholic, Protestant and Reform Jewish faiths.

Although the decision of next of kin takes precedence over the written wishes of prospective organ donors, in some states the wishes of the deceased to donate his/her body take legal precedence over those of next of kin. (Anatomy departments are not inclined to accept a body over objections to donation, however.) It is advisable for potential donors to talk their decision over with family members and resolve differences well in advance of that time when such final decisions must be made under the handicap of grief.

Requirements vary

Every anatomy department has its own set of rules and regulations. Below are some of the variations:

- Some will receive bodies from which organs have been donated, some will not.

- Others need tissue that has not been "set" with embalming.
- Often anatomy departments insist on doing their own embalming.
- A few have limited donor enrollment and accept only on an "as needed" basis.
- Occasionally, next-of-kin donations are not permitted.

Upon request, medical schools will send Consent and Information forms which must be completed and witnessed (preferably by family members), and returned to the facility. A photocopy of the form is then returned to the donor, along with a wallet card to be carried at all times. The donor should mark the back of his drivers license.

The donor may specify the particular medical school with which he is registered as recipient, or, in case death occurs out of state, permission may be given to arrange donation there. Most states' departments of anatomy jurisdiction does not extend more than 50 miles beyond state lines, and the family will be responsible for expenses involved in transportation beyond that jurisdiction. Donor registration may be canceled at any time or transferred to another state in case of residence change.

When death occurs, the receiving institution should be notified immediately. Certain information must be obtained before the body will be deemed acceptable. Bodies may be refused for donation if the person was severely injured in an accident; suffering from a contagious disease such as hepatitis at the time of death; grossly overweight or severely emaciated; profoundly deformed; or if the body was autopsied. Because the body may be refused, it is wise for prospective donors to make contingent funeral plans.

Bodies used for instruction of medical students must be preserved for a much longer time than the few days usually required for a conventional funeral, and arterial embalming is required. If the donor dies in a hospital with in-house morgue, the anatomy department may offer to retrieve the body and perform the embalming to its own specifications at no charge. If the donor dies at home or in a hospital without a morgue, the family may call on a funeral home to do the special embalming. The cost varies, but averages around $300. This cost alone is borne by the family. The body will not be available for the funeral or memorial service.

Body donation can be pre-arranged by any person 18 years old or older. Family members may also consent to donate the body of a loved one at the time of death. Unless the decedent has made an un-revoked refusal to make an anatomical gift, the following classes of persons, in order of priority, may make an anatomical gift of the decedent of any age: spouse; adult son or daughter; either parent; adult brother or sister; grandparent; guardian at the time of death.

"This is the place where death rejoices to come to the aid of life."

—Quotation found in autopsy rooms worldwide

Entire body donation is the ultimate unselfish gift to science and the future of mankind. It can also be a final gift to a family already financially burdened and fatigued by days or weeks of difficult decision-making and grief.

Chapter Six

Planning Today's Funeral: How We Say Good-bye

Ellie is a lively 75-year-old. Everyone in the community admires her good disposition and her yard full of flowers. Recovering from a mild stroke she suffered in the fall, Ellie realizes that spring gardening takes more out of her than it used to. Her husband is long dead, and her only son is estranged and living across the country. Being a take-charge kind of person, Ellie decides to take the initiative and pre-arrange her own funeral. It won't be easy, but she's cared for herself and all her business dealings for years. Why leave those final important decisions to chance? Ellie is about to get an education she hadn't expected.

Pre-arrange or pre-pay

Ellie is luckier than most people planning a funeral. She isn't in the throes of deep sorrow, nor has she spent days or even weeks at the bedside of a loved one. Each year in America, over two million families must make some sort of funeral arrangements, and most must decide on lasting choices in an extremely short time, under the worst possible conditions. Their task will be easier if some degree of prior planning has taken place. The greater amount of prior planning, the less responsibility falls on grieving family members.

Many thoughtful people pre-arrange or pre-pay for their own funerals. A distinction must be made between the two terms. **Pre-arrangement** includes planning and making selections which are recorded and kept on file by a funeral home for use when it becomes necessary to carry out those plans. **Pre-payment** entails also paying for chosen goods and services at present market value with the anticipation that the buyer's wishes will be honored.

Questions to ask

Certain questions should be asked before pre-paying for a funeral:

- Is the money tied up in an account or policy earning less than the market rate?
- Will the plan keep pace with inflation?
- Is there a price guarantee?
- Can the policy be canceled, and is there a penalty for doing so?
- Can the agreement be used only at a particular funeral home or chain?
- Can the policy be moved to another funeral home, even another state?
- Is the seller licensed or registered?

Visit the facility

Don't depend on good faith in dealing with a person making a door-to-door or telephone sales pitch. If there is any cause for concern, check with the Better Business Bureau, the State Insurance Commissioner, or Attorney General.

Pre-need planning is a good idea, and it is big business, according to a 1995 AARP survey. Almost 17 million adults age 50 and over had prepaid some, or all, of their funeral and/or burial expenses, and the practice is growing.

If a need is felt to make financial arrangements, consider a Totten Trust. The consumer controls the individual savings plan, opens the account and deposits a sum of trust or money equal to the cost of the funeral in a passbook savings account, or he may secure a Certificate of Deposit (CD). Interest on the money should keep up with inflation. The account or CD is earmarked for funeral costs, and the owner asks a banker or lawyer to draw up a formal Totten Trust agreement which provides that the money be released at the time of need.

Pre-planning late in life

In pre-planning a funeral late in life, it is well to select favorite clothing and accessories, and it is a good idea to include a color photograph to assist the cosmetologist with hair style and make-up (this applies to both men and women). Most funeral homes will not take responsibility for keeping articles of clothing unless death is imminent. Informing a close friend or relative about the selected garments and their whereabouts is adequate. Names, addresses, and phone numbers of pall bearers and a list of younger alternates will be invaluable to the funeral director, whose job it is to secure them. While this information is often kept with a will, it is best left with the funeral director as part of pre-arrangement.

The evolution of final arrangements

Final arrangements have changed over time in this country. Early American colonists followed much the same rituals and practices that they remembered from their countries of origin. From homemade coffins and diverse religious services dictated by society, practices evolved through manufactured caskets and standardized funerals until today, choice of burial and final ceremonies have become as unique as the individual being memorialized.

Embalming began during the Civil War and did not become a commonly accepted practice until after the turn of the century.

First funeral homes

The first funeral homes were furniture stores where coffins were sold, then residences were converted to funeral homes. Later, storefront buildings were replaced by buildings constructed for the sole purpose of providing undertaking, visitation, and funeral services. In some cases, funeral directors now serve the family for several months following a funeral, filing necessary claims for Social Security payments and veterans' benefits.

Before making any plans, a talk with clergy and a visit to several funeral homes and cemeteries may be in order. Attending a number of last rites and burials may have formed a favorable opinion about particular ones, thus limiting the need for comparison shopping.

When planning, choices must first be made about the final resting place of the body. Although above-ground entombment in a mausoleum is an alternative, interment, or earth burial, is the most popular form of burial (see Chapter Eight). In recent years, cremation has gained acceptance, and today, 21% of Americans choose cremation (see Chapter Seven).

FTC Regulations

When either pre-arranging or pre-paying, the Federal Trade Commission (FTC) has ruled that funeral homes must make available to the consumer a price list detailing all goods and services and varying grades of same. There are many subtle sales tactics of which the consumer must be wary, but he will be in a much more rational state of mind than relatives will be at the time of need.

Keeping in mind that the average cost of a funeral in this country today is $5,500 and climbing, cost is a consideration. The funeral business began as a hardware store sideline where coffins were built on demand, and it slowly grew as entrepreneurs "undertook" to furnish goods needed for mourning and burial. It has grown to a $16 billion-a-year industry. The death-care trade's one-stop shopping has become both a convenience and a trap. Marketing abuses were cited by Jessica Mitford in her 1963 book, *The American Way of Death*, and reforms instituted by the FTC regarding pricing and sales practices resulted from her expose'. The regulations the FTC made in 1984 were largely designed to "lower barriers to price competition in the funeral market and facilitate informed consumer choice."

A funeral is the third most expensive single purchase most consumers ever make, after their home and car.

Caution: the funeral home you and your family have trusted for a lifetime may now be owned by a funeral chain. Though it bears the same familiar name and many of the same people still work there, consumers must exercise the same caution necessary in dealing with an unfamiliar provider.

Basic services

Regardless of the type or cost of the funeral selected, the funeral home's basic services include:

- Transportation of the body from the place of death.
- Consultation with the family and preparation of documents and notices associated with the death
- Care of the body before disposition
- Preparation of the body if ceremony and burial are chosen
- Location and direction of visitations and funeral service
- Transportation to church, if church ceremony is desired, or to crematory if cremation is selected
- Use of funeral home vehicles such as hearse, limousines and cars for the family

Funeral products and goods include:
- Casket
- A variety of vaults or concrete grave liners (although not required by law, many cemeteries require these to prevent the grave's sinking)
- Register books, acknowledgment cards, and funeral programs, and, in some cases, burial clothing
- Incidental costs such as fees for pallbearers, honoraria for clergy, music, and obituary
- Equipment such as tents and chairs for grave-side services

Selecting the casket

The largest single expenditure is for the casket. This item makes the difference between a moderately priced and an expensive funeral. Prices range from below $1,000 for a cloth-covered casket, to around $10,000 for a bronze one. Prices can go considerably higher for specially made coffins, such as the gold-plated over bronze, which looks like solid gold, for $26,000.

Selecting a casket is a highly personal experience and sometimes a family is pressured into easy payment plans at a time when their grief overcomes their ability to recognize what they can afford. If pre-arrangement has not been made, designate in writing which family members are responsible for making the decisions concerning the casket and funeral home. For more information on selecting a funeral home contact:

>National Funeral Directors Association
>13625 Bishop's Drive
>Brookfield, WI 53005
>(800) 228-6332
>http://www.nfda.org

Memorial societies

The American style of last rites is the most elaborate and costly in the world. Added to that, "the emotional trauma of bereavement, the lack of information, and time pressures place the consumer at an enormous disadvantage in making funeral arrangements," according to a nationwide survey made by the Federal Trade Commission (FTC). In reaction to what some perceive as excesses surrounding last rites, **memorial societies** have come into being.

A memorial society is an association of consumers who want a simple but dignified funeral. Rich or poor, members reject increasingly expensive and complicated services. Membership is inexpensive and the organizations are non-profit, non-sectarian, and geared to help people make practical funeral plans. They take some of the mystery out of funeral arrangements. Recently some commercial enterprises have adopted the word "society" in their name, so caution must be exercised. Check the Yellow Pages of the phone directory to find memorial societies in your area or write:

>Funeral and Memorial Societies of America (FAMSA)
>P.O. Box 10
>Hinesburg, VT 05461
>802-482-3431
>http://www.funerals.org/famsa

Benefits

Membership benefits include:

- Literature and information on a wide range of less expensive funeral options. In most states, family members can carry out many funeral arrangements without a funeral director.
- Provisions and agreements with one or more undertakers who offer tasteful yet inexpensive options at a nominal cost.
- A pre-arrangement form which allows members to make a detailed funeral plan. This can be changed or canceled at will—the pre-arrangement form is not a legal contract, it is an expression of the member's wishes.
- Availability of up-to-date information concerning legal requirements so that personal decisions are based on accurate information. This includes current funeral practices and state and federal legislation.

While memorial society members come from all walks of life, they have something in common—they feel that money spent on expensive funerals would be better spent on the living. Most prefer the following:

- No embalming. The Center for Disease Control (CDC) states that embalming serves no public health service. No state routinely requires embalming, though some require embalming or refrigeration after 24-48 hours especially if the body is to be shipped out of state.
- A simple service. A memorial service without the body present or a grave-side service are often preferred.
- A low-cost coffin. The St. Francis Burial and Counseling Society goes so far as to furnish instructions for building

a coffin, the pine box of the not-too-distant past. For detailed instructions on building a coffin write:

The St. Francis Center
135 MacArthur Blvd. N.W.
Washington, D.C. 20016

Pre-arrangement

Pre-arrangement gives an individual the opportunity to make these decisions. Memorial society membership is transferable among all societies in the U.S. and Canada for little or no charge. A nominal lifetime membership fee of $10 to $30 per individual or family and sometimes a small annual renewal fee ensure a means of making thoughtful and affordable final choices.

Ours is the only country in which the practice of embalming is widely promoted. It is rarely done in other countries, with no risk to public health.

Traditional services built entirely around a person's religious faith have given way to more informal and creative ceremonies. Services started taking on new forms when people begin dying at an early age as a result of AIDS and other terminal illnesses that afforded time for choosing more personalized services.

Alvin Toffler, author of Future Shock, *points out that because of the great amount of change taking place in American life, rituals surrounding birth, death and marriage become "change buffers" which keep change from becoming disturbingly chaotic.*

Today the tone is less of deep grief and sorrow and more of what the industry terms the "life appreciation service." These services are highly individualized, with upbeat eulogies and music that helps those who have suffered a loss to become more able to accept life without the loved one. Popular music is woven in with hymns, memorabilia is displayed at family visitations, and professionally produced videos memorializing the deceased have become part of the service. Either a lay person or clergy or a combination of both may officiate.

Later on, there are many highly personalized ways for close friends and family to honor their loved one. A person who was appreciated for his or her cooking ability may be honored by compiling favorite recipes into a booklet to be sent to close friends and family members. A person known for flamboyant creations of art work or clothing might be remembered by having their work distributed among those closest to them.

Of course, the traditional funeral remains and is the most appropriate form for many, but any effort to comfort those left behind may be viewed as progress.

Chapter Seven

Cremation: Leaving the Land for the Living

Frank and Lila are the last of their respective families. Neither has siblings—a reflection of the scaled-back families of the late 1920s. Their few remaining cousins live in distant states, and a career as musicians with no desire for children leaves them anchorless in their retirement. Each has requested that the other hire a jazz band to play at his or her memorial service, and neither sees any logic in having a grave site that no one will visit. Their matter-of-fact lifestyle doesn't lend itself to funerary tradition. Both have chosen cremation and inurnment in an outdoor columbarium.

Making the choice

Frank and Lila are not alone in their choice. Twenty-one percent of Americans opt for cremation, up from around 4% in the early 1960's. It has been said that in a mobile society, only the dead stay put. Today's fast-paced lifestyles have broken with all customs from birth to death, and more and more often, people are choosing not to stay put after death.

One person said, "When I looked at the options, the ones that cremation offer far outweigh what you can do in a permanent, meaningless place." So much for cemeteries.

Another said of plans for scattering her cremains, "There's a romance to it. Some of my remains will be in places that were very meaningful to me."

Cremation rates are highest in mobile populations — 54% in Nevada where few have a home church or cemetery. In San Francisco, 80% of Caucasians choose cremation.

Hispanics, African-Americans, and Asians still hold to traditional rituals, and those from the deep South are less likely to desert conventional burial. The importance of "where you're from, a sense of place and belonging," is reflected in the numbers. Only 4% choose cremation in Alabama.

A history of honor

Although all cultures honor their dead, the means employed by one may appear to be a desecration by another.

> *Throughout human history man has employed ritual behavior to deal with critical moments... I know of no people for whom the fact of death is not critical, and who have no ritual by which to deal with it.*
> —*Anthropologist Margaret Mead*

The practice of cremation has a long and varied history. Charred human bones dating about 1800 BC were found at the Neolithic site of Stonehenge in England. In the Early Iron Age (around 1000 BC.), cremation spread widely. At a time of importance of gold, silver, bronze, and iron smelting, people felt that intense fire separated the soul from the bodily dross during cremation, sending it heavenward. Vikings justified huge funeral pyres believing that the higher the smoke rose into the air, the higher the person's soul would rise.

At around that same time, the custom spread, and Greeks involved in distant wars began the practice of bringing the ashes of their battle heroes home. For five centuries beginning in 400 BC, cremation was the normal method used by Romans for disposing of their dead. As funeral pyres became more elaborate and therefore more expensive, they became the privilege of royalty, and ordinary citizens could not afford the fuel. Therefore, earth burial became preferred by the masses for economic reasons well before Christianity influenced their choice.

Because of the Christian faith's teaching of resurrection of the dead, as the religion spread, cremation fell into disfavor. It was also partly a reaction to its being a Roman custom.

After evidence was found that burial grounds were frequently at the center of epidemics of cholera and other contagious diseases, the practice of cremation was championed for sanitary reasons. Although criticized as "anti-Christian," in 1880, over a hundred members of the British Medical Association signed a petition to the government in favor of cremation. It was at that time that the need for death certification was mandated, since there was no body to examine in case foul play became suspected. It was decreed that two practitioners must sign a form which indicated that traces of criminal death were absent.

Cremation in America

In 1920, there were only 13,000 cremations in the United States, less than 1% of the deaths that year. Then in the early 1960's Jessica Mitford's *American Way of Death* and Ruth Harmer's

High Cost of Dying allowed the public to look behind the pall surrounding funeral home practices. Many consumers reacted by looking for alternatives, and that trend continues.

Jessica Mitford took a parting shot at expensive traditional funerals when, at her death in 1996, she chose direct cremation for a reported cost of $562.31.

Final rites have always been closely associated with prevailing religious belief. During the 1963 Vatican II Council, Pope Paul VI issued a decree removing some of the penalties against Christians who practiced cremation, and today cremation is permitted on grounds of national custom, economy, and hygiene. Most Protestant churches now approve of it, although there is lagging acceptance in America's Bible Belt. In New York, funeral homes report that nearly half of their cremation business is Catholic, and in California and figure approaches 75%. Eighty percent of the world's population now lives in cultures where cremation is not prohibited, and cremation is encouraged for about half the people on the globe.

In the last 20 years, cremations have increased to 250,000 annually in the U.S., whereas burials have only increased by about 60,000 a year. By 2010, it is estimated that the number of cremations will increase 200%.

Practicality is perhaps the leading reason for choosing cremation. With the current average cost of $8,000 for a traditional funeral, burial, and marker, it is an option that must be considered. Total cost of direct cremation can range from as low as $300 to as much as $2,000.

The Federal Funeral Rule requires that funeral directors must seek permission before they embalm a body because when destined for direct cremation or direct burial, embalming is not necessary. Funeral directors urge and most families agree that embalming should take place if an open casket funeral is planned.

Cremation costs

A direct cremation is usually arranged through a funeral home, but in some states it can be arranged through direct contact with a crematory. The consumer needs to be aware of basic services which include:
- Transportation of the body to the funeral home and/or crematory
- Care of the body for the period of hours required by state regulations (one or more days)
- Services of the funeral director, if through a funeral home
- Purchase of an alternative container as required by state law; these containers are made of cardboard, fiberboard, or plywood at a cost that should not exceed $150.

Over 100 varieties of urns are on the market for as little as $20 for a plastic one to as much as $3,500 for a 24K gold-plated one encrusted with sapphires. Batesville Casket, the country's largest casket maker, markets "keepsake urns," five inches high, to encourage people to divide the ashes among-family members.

The type ceremony desired to precede or follow cremation is another factor to be considered. A funeral can be held with the body present (with cremation following) , but the cost can come close to that of a traditional funeral because of added services provided by the funeral home (see Chapter Six for funerals).

Rental caskets can dramatically reduce the expense of a funeral service followed by cremation. Ceremonial caskets rent from $600 to $800, and after the service, the lining of the casket is replaced (at least one state, Massachusetts, prohibits the use of rental caskets for health reasons). Federal law prohibits a funeral director from requiring that a "real" casket be purchased for cremation.

Rental caskets are available, but it is necessary for the family to inquire about them because they are unpopular with funeral directors. Cremation is also unpopular because its increasing acceptance cuts into undertaking establishments' share of the $16 billion per year funeral business.

Cremation versus burial

In the past five years, funeral prices have risen faster than the cost of living. Knowing that mourners do not shop around at the time of need is one of the trade's "attractive industry fundamentals." The consumer must be aware of necessary and unnecessary services and accompanying expenses.

There's one thing in this world which a person don't say: "I'll look around a little, and if I find I can't do better I'll come back and take it." That's a coffin.
—*Mark Twain*

In this country, a death occurs about every 16 seconds. There are currently two million acres in the U.S. dedicated to graveyards. If the present death rate continues, congested urban areas will want their space used by the living, and many view ground burial as impractical, as in land-scarce countries such as England and Denmark. In densely populated Japan, cremation is required in Tokyo, and cremation is the method of body disposal for around 95% of the population.

Each of us should seriously consider the benefits to humanity of cremation... The living need open space ... The soul is not anchored to a tombstone or a tiny plot of ground.
—*Former Secretary of Interior, Walter Hickel*

Memorial services

If direct cremation is chosen, a formal church memorial may be scheduled or an informal memorial may be planned. Although the crematory may have a small chapel, an informal memorial at a place meaningful to the deceased may be more therapeutic for family and friends.

Some who made their wishes known in choosing cremation may also have suggested the type service he/she wished to have. Leaving choices to others may seem a passive relinquishment of control or it may be perceived as leaving an unnecessary burden on survivors. Many believe that death-style like life-style is a form of self-expression.

The memorial service offers a more relaxed occasion than conventional funeral rites with their obituary-like recitation of life history. Focus on the well-lived life through many short tributes is more supportive than one or two long eulogies.

> *Planning such an event should be a job of honor for someone close to the deceased but not in the immediate family. The service . . . should last about an hour. A subdued social gathering after the service, which is an adaptation of the pre-burial wake, is another innovation of which Miss Manners approves.*
> —*Columnist Judith Martin (Miss Manners)*

Scattering ashes

Still another alternative is the scattering of ashes. There are restrictions governing the practice, however:

- In National Parks and on most private land, it is considered littering.
- On private property that isn't your own, you need permission.
- Streams, rivers, and lakes are usually off limits, as are beaches.
- Under Environmental Protection Agency rules, ocean scatterings must take place at least three nautical miles off shore.

Most coastal states have charter boats which advertise "seamations." A few states have laws prohibiting this choice of disposition.

Colorado's "Angel of the Ashes," a woman pilot, scatters ashes from 600 to 800 feet. When ashes are dispersed, they resemble a jet trail. She then flies back over the area and rocks the plane's wings as she leaves.

If you choose to scatter Uncle Jack around his favorite golf course or fishing hole, you may not be discovered, and if you are, chances are that you'll get nothing more than a scolding. As one creative director of a consumer cremation group said, "It's easier too ask forgiveness than get permission."

Cremation is cheaper than conventional burial, even if the deceased chooses to be shot into space. In December of 1996, the cremains of 20 people were launched on a U.S. satellite. Once in space, the rocket jettisoned a container holding their encapsulated ashes. The container was expected to orbit earth for about two years, reenter the atmosphere, and vaporize with a fiery burst. Two of the late fellow travelers were Gene Roddenberry and the ultimate space cadet, Timothy Leary. Cost—$4,800 per capsule.

Resources

For further information about cremation visit the web site: or write the National Cremation Society, P.O. Box 3696, Holiday, Florida, 34690-0676, (800) 370-0020, http://www.ncs-fl.com.

Chapter Eight

Cemeteries, Mausoleums, and Columbaria: Down to Earth or Heart-Level

Like most men who served in World War II, Charlie's life is defined by his years in service. He has never again had that sense of purpose, that feeling of camaraderie shared by men whose lives depended on each other. Every other year when the crew of his Navy destroyer holds its reunion, a few more "deck apes" are missing, but those still standing beside their war brides stiffen their backs and salute as they hear the names of deceased comrades. Too often, Charlie finds himself saying goodbye at the confluence of ordered rows of white crosses. Somehow, the quiet, the regimented order of a national cemetery symbolizes the peace they all fought for. Charlie has decided that it would be nice to have taps echoing in the pines above his final resting place.

Evolution of the American cemetery

Like all things military, there are rules, regulations, and guarantees. Charlie knows without question that perpetual care and honor will be assured at the national cemetery of his choice. Municipal and privately owned cemeteries are another story. This is the least regulated sector of the death industry.

The traditional American cemetery in the 18th and early 19th centuries was set amid the living in the middle of town, as in the churchyard where burial was restricted to members of the congregation.

In the 19th century, as government authorities recognized health hazards of such locations and as space limitations grew more acute, cemeteries were moved to the outskirts of town. Gradually, municipalities began to assume more responsibility for burial grounds and enact laws and regulations to govern them.

Regulation of sales

All states have laws regulating cemeteries, but some do not make clear distinctions between public, private, profit, non-profit, and those owned by organizations. Some corporations which sell cemetery lots are organized in states that have lax control over sales. They then sell lots in other states from the parent company. Some state laws are ineffective in securing public disclosure of records of complex, pyramidal corporate structures and are therefore unable to police sales policies.

Across the U.S., this hit-or-miss regulation is carried out by a different governing body in every location (and only for-profit cemeteries are regulated). Sometimes the State Cemetery Board, or the State Securities Department will require registration and scrutiny, while in some states, cemetery issues have never been addressed. The primary concern is that an adequate amount of money will be placed in trust to provide perpetual care for the grounds.

This is one area in which long-term planning can take place, but the consumer must proceed with caution. After conferring with the prospective buyer, the cemetery salesperson establishes the number of lots needed (some cemeteries sell lots in multiples of two), and during a tour of the grounds, shows available sites. In pre-need purchases, a down payment of 20% is required with monthly payments for the next two to three years. Ten percent of the lot's price goes into a trust fund to provide perpetual care. It is important to have this guaranteed, because if upkeep is not included in the cost, an annual fee will be assessed in perpetuity.

Provisions of ownership

Usually, the cemetery lot owner does not acquire freehold right (absolute ownership) in the land, but only an easement entitling interment of the number of bodies the deed provides, subject to the regulations of the cemetery or public authorities as applicable.

A prospective buyer should ascertain whether funds in the cemetery under consideration are sufficient to maintain a plot or crypt. The buyer may want to contact the appropriate state agency about provision of endowment care of the cemetery property. Also, check grave sites to see how they are being maintained. Ask if only the cemetery's markers and services can be used—outside purchases may have an added charge placed on them.

Some cemeteries may add the cost of their own monuments or markers to the plot sale. They may add a further charge saying a vault is required. This requirement is not a city or state law, it is a regulation of that particular cemetery. The justification is that otherwise graves would sink. They may also require flat markers flush with the ground for ease in mowing the grounds.

There is a need to beware of pre-need scams. Don't purchase lots by telephone without seeing the cemetery, and do be sure to buy from a reputable company. Otherwise, you may find many years later that the firm has gone out of business, and that the new owner/firm refuses to honor the previous owner's contracts.

Beware that cemeteries have different rules about resale of lots. In some cases, lots may not be sold for profit, and some can only be sold through a cemetery broker for a fee. Some cemeteries do not allow plots to be sold at all, and if the purchaser moves far away, survivors will be burdened with the cost of transporting the body back from the place of death.

When economy is important, remember that almost every locality has at least one cemetery that does not required a vault. Also note that burial costs may be higher in the late afternoon, on weekends and holidays. Many cemeteries have religious or ethnic restrictions.

Crypts and mausoleums

Embalming is required before entombment in above-ground crypts and mausoleums. A special casket which can be properly sealed is required and a sealed metal coffin with manufacturer's warranty attending to construction is sometimes required. If not metal, the coffin may have to be placed within a metal vault.

After entombment, the marble facing is put permanently into place, complete with inscription. Inscriptions on crypts are sometimes subject to approval of the management, and there are often restrictions on placing flowers, wreaths, plants, and vases at the crypt.

There are also underground and lawn crypts called turf-top crypts. Pre-poured concrete chambers or pre-cast boxes are installed side by side for multiple bodies, which are then covered with earth and sod.

Markers and monuments

Flat markers are often used in urban areas, but in rural areas, monuments (tombstones) are still preferred. Advertisers for markers tell consumers they should get away from the traditional "marble orchard" and the depressing aspects of cold, cold stone.

Grave stones may be purchased from monument retailers or

from cemeteries. Some funeral directors sell them for the convenience of the families they serve. Bronze markers range in price from about $500, and upright monuments are priced from $1,800, including die and base. The cost can be considerably higher depending on size and craftsmanship of the memorial. Monuments are installed in concrete grounding.

Housing cremains

Mausoleums offer cubicles approximately 12" x 12" x 12", some of which have glass fronts. A mausoleum niche, including inurnment and engraving, costs around $1,000.

There are no federal or state requirements for an "urn vault." If the consumer purchases his own urn, there should be no "inspection fee." However, cemeteries are permitted to set their own policies, and consumers can do little about them.

A **columbarium** is a building made to house only cremains. The word columbarium is derived from the Latin *columba*, which means dove. The dovecote, or nesting area, is made up of many niches where doves make their homes. Therefore, a columbarium consists of a number of recessed niches, either indoors or outdoors, to hold cremation urns. Note: Cremains can be sent by mail or private carrier such as UPS.

National cemeteries

In 1995, veteran deaths totaled 513,000 annually, while in 1997, they climbed to 537,000. They are expected to peak in 2008, at 620,000. Twenty percent of eligible Vietnam veterans are requesting burial in national cemeteries compared with 9.3% of World War II veterans. This means that burial in a national cemetery is a serious option for many. Compare the information already provided in this chapter, and the reader will see why.

Burial benefits in a Veterans Affairs national cemetery include the grave site, opening and closing of the grave, and perpetual care. Many cemeteries have columbaria for the inurnment of cremated remains or special grave sites for the burial of cremated remains. Headstones and markers and placement are provided at government expense. Cemeteries for veterans are also operated by many states. To request the VA pamphlet entitled *Federal Benefits for Veterans and Dependents,* or for other information, contact the Interior Department or the respective states. For a list of available cemeteries see Appendix or contact:

U.S. Dept. of Veterans Affairs
Washington, D.C. 20420
800-827-1000
http://www.va.gov

Eligibility requirements

A veteran and spouse should be aware of the location of the veteran's discharge and separation papers. If these papers cannot be found, duplicate copies may be obtained by contacting the National Personnel Records Center, Military Personnel Records, 9700 Page Blvd., St. Louis, MO 63132-5100. The veteran's full name should be printed clearly, but the request must also contain the veteran's signature or the signature of the next of kin, if the veteran is deceased. Use the Standard Form 180, Request Pertaining to Military Records which is available from VA offices.

Spouses and dependent, minor children of eligible veterans and of armed forces members also may be buried in a national cemetery. Grave sites cannot be reserved. Funeral directors or others making burial arrangements must apply at the time of death.

The VA provides headstones and markers for the graves of veterans anywhere in the world and for eligible dependents of veterans buried in national, state veterans, or federal cemeteries. Flat bronze, flat granite, flat marble and upright marble types are available consistent with existing monuments at the place of burial. Niche markers are also available for use in columbaria.

When burial occurs in a cemetery other than a national cemetery or state veterans cemetery, the headstone or marker must be applied for through the VA. Although it is shipped at government expense, VA does not pay the cost of placement at grave sites. Forms and assistance are available at VA regional offices. The VA will also pay the cost of transporting the remains of a service-disabled veteran to the national cemetery nearest the home of the deceased.

Chapter Nine

Bereavement, Grief, and the State of Mourning: Easing the Pain

Carolyne married her high school sweetheart two weeks after graduation. After forty happy years of marriage, his fatal heart attack turned her life into an uninterrupted cry of anguish. Her children and friends tell her that time will diminish the pain, and the books they've given her about grief even name the feelings and phases she must pass through— a timetable of sorts. She feels guilty and confused because her sorrow follows no familiar pattern, it is omnipresent and endless. Managing a household and paying bills was daunting: now preparing to file income tax is insurmountable. How can she go on when just getting out of bed requires all the energy she can muster? Inner strength isn't going to be enough.

The changing perception of grief

Carolyne remembers a time when widows wore black for a prescribed period of time, and subdued behavior was expected of them. There were many mourning customs that offered a framework, a boundary, an overt means of expressing sorrow. Without a word being said, these customs indicated that here is a person in need of extra concern and comfort from others.

As our culture became less tradition-bound, the rigid grief customs have given way to bereavement that consists of understanding and working through the grieving process. Each individual is seen to need emotional resources to cope with his or her particular loss.

Grief may be strong or weak, brief or prolonged, immediate or delayed. Grief is the experience of deep or violent sorrow; mourning is the expression of that sorrow.

Yet care of the bereaved is still a communal responsibility. Family members and friends are invaluable in their ability to be sensitive and sympathetic. Some may fail to realize that the bereaved person is in a period of ongoing mourning, and as a person begins to cope and enters again the land of the living, many withdraw support. Consistency is needed. Knowing that there are those who are constant, who are not going to disappear,is a necessity. Grief must be shared. The normal mourning process requires talking with good listeners— reminiscence is a very real part of grieving.

Sometimes we confuse sadness with depression, replace comfort with Prozac. We expect, maybe insist, upon an end to grief. Trauma, pain, detachment, acceptance in a year—Time's up.

—*Ellen Goodman*

Bereavement

A readiness to investigate a person's feelings of loss, and the willingness to determine why they feel as they do can often shine the light of understanding on emotional suffering that appears to be without end. Life is a series of losses—loss of jobs, loss of familiar places, friends, and traditions. How we deal with any of these will, in a small way, predict how we will cope with great loss.

Learning to recognize the signposts of bereavement and to realize which of these unfamiliar behaviors is normal and which will require outside help to overcome can take some of the uncertainty and much unrealistic expectation out of the long and deeply felt process.

Loss of a spouse

A man's dying is more the survivor's affair than his own.
— *Thomas Mann*

Loss of a spouse is usually the most traumatic and disruptive event in a person's life. The first response to a great and sudden loss is shock, described by some as numbness, an emotional state that serves as a coping mechanism. It is in essence detachment of logical thought from feelings and may last from a short while to days or weeks of "holding up" until the emotional impact finally breaks through and grieving begins.

When the bereaved begins to face the sadness and loneliness of his new state of being, he may use many strategies to relieve his pain. He may engage in frenetic activity to the point of exhausting his already depleted energy. He may engage in self-destructive behavior such as over-indulgence in food or alcohol. A grieving person's resistance is low, and his reasoning ranges from "why not?" and "who cares?" to "I've been through so much, I'm entitled."

This is a time to take special care of physical and emotional health. Bereavement may be fatal. One study has shown an increase of almost 40% in the death rate of widowers over the age of 54 during the first six months of bereavement. Another study found that 4.8% died within the first year of bereavement compared with 0.7% of a comparable group of non-bereaved people.

The battle within may run the gamut from anger (at the dead spouse for the lifestyle that caused his/her death; over residual wrongs in the relationship; at being left alone to face life's responsibilities), to anxiety (over uncertainty of the future and concerns about the children), to guilt (accompanying a sense of relief for the deceased as well as the bereaved after a long illness).

The fight for survival includes changes in ability to function (health risks due to suppressed immune functions, mental disorganization, confusion and memory disturbances); altered family relationships (helping young children with their grief, helping surviving parents grieve, and dealing with expectations of older children), and a changed role in society (lack of acceptance by couples, attempts at intimacy and sexuality accompanied by feelings of betrayal and guilt).

Underlying all these feelings is a change in personal identity. A dependent spouse (of either sex) may be overwhelmed by the new perception of himself as single rather than part of a couple, and as totally responsible for his own life and well-being and often that of others. Even his/her religious and philosophical views may have been undermined or drastically altered by the death of one so close, so indispensable. The bereaved person is often left with his belief system shaken.

Depression

One frequent response to such a loss is depression, which literally means, "forced downward." Common symptoms are feelings of hopelessness; insomnia or early wakening; thoughts of suicide; irritability; loss of appetite; fatigue and decreased energy;

inability to think or concentrate; and absence of pleasure in activities formerly enjoyed. There may be a legitimate need for drugs, but this need should be physician-supervised and brief.

The definition of depression is any person who is unhappy and ill with his unhappiness.

One theory is that after a deep loss, descent into depression is necessary because dismantling old patterns and interactions is necessary in order for new patterns and interactions to emerge. Sometimes professional help is required in order that the depression does not become so deep that the person cannot pull out of it physically or mentally. In such cases a professional can lead the bereaved person through this period of suffering in a more orderly fashion with less disruption to his or her life.

Return to a former state can be only partial, never complete. Things are never the same.

There must be an evolution of identity, a changing from the other-oriented part of a couple to an individual. A healthy adaptation to the death involves a new relationship and its integration into the changing life of the bereaved. Early in the grief process, the grieving person must find an altered relationship with the dead spouse, sustained by ongoing dreams, memories, and living legacies.

Almost everyone experiences some kind strange phenomenon following the loss of a loved one.
—*Elizabeth Harper Neeld, Ph.D.*

Variables that affect the intensity and length of the grieving process depend greatly on many factors including:

- the grieving person's personality
- his/her previous way of dealing with loss

- the importance of the lost person to the griever's life structure
- circumstances surrounding the death
- the amount and type of support offered by friends and family
- the difficulty of the circumstances surrounding the grieving person
- unresolved conflicts with the person lost

All mourners share certain characteristics. Mourners of all types of losses are confused by unexpected feelings and feelings thought to be inappropriate and therefore not to be "owned." Such feelings include a sense of:

- injustice (It isn't fair for one so young to die.)
- guilt (She was more worthy than I to live/If I had only paid more attention to her symptoms.)
- anger (The whole family must pay for his selfish lifestyle.)
- helplessness (I depended on him for everything.)
- illogic (Parents were not meant to out-live their children.)
- ambivalence (So much suffering—do I feel relief for myself or for her?)

Phyllis Silverman, co-director of a study at Massachusetts General Hospital in Boston, contrasts the male and female model of loss. Mourners who follow the male model want to "get on with life," become involved in work and other activities. However, the female model recognizes the need for connection rather than disengagement and separation. Those who follow the male model are said to change their ties with the past, not necessarily to break them, and they often need help in learning to reconnect and relate after a loss, while those who adopt the female model may need to learn independence and how to take care of themselves. Depending on the personality and nature of the relationship of the person lost to the one left behind, the male model may be assumed by a grieving female while the female model may be chosen by a man.

Loss of a child

If loss of a spouse is the most disruptive event in a person's life, loss of a child is the most tragic and long lasting. A natural pattern has been broken, and the unfairness of the loss intensifies the sorrow that must be borne.

It has been speculated that, with smaller families and with less expectation of loss of a child, we are not only less prepared for such a loss, but there is greater attachment for each child. All will agree that, no matter the size of the family, the death of any one of the children is a crushing loss. Parents lose not only the child but the expectations they held for them and for themselves.

Affects on the marriage and family

It is very important for parents to communicate their true feelings to each other. Men often hold in their grief for fear of totally losing control if they let go. But withheld grief is like water behind a dam, and at some point that dam will break. This stoicism may be perceived by the wife and mother as lack of feeling. There is nothing that can eliminate the pain associated with the loss of a child, but communication between parents can help them express this grief in a healthy way.

Grandparents suffer a double heartache. They have grief feelings for both the dead grandchild and their own sorrowing child.

Some parents behave in a way they feel they are expected to by other people, "What would people say if. . . ?" and continue mourning long after they should start breaking out of their grief pattern.

If you feel uncomfortable at the sight of youngsters laughing and playing, if this sight fills you with envy or bitterness, know that many bereaved parents have felt the same.

Resumption of sexual intercourse, an embodiment of pleasure, can cause one partner to see the other as an "insatiable animal" when he/she may be reaching for closeness. For some who are unable to express grief openly, sex represents a brief release from the pain of grief.

Bereaved parents face two diametrically opposite responses from friends. One grieving parent felt people "don't want to talk to us, as if what happened to us will rub off on them." Another found that "everyone who has lost a child wants to tell me in great detail of their own suffering. That's not what I need to hear."

Parents should be cautioned about the devastating effect continued grief has on surviving siblings. It can make these children feel as if they mean nothing to their parents. By idealizing the dead child, it makes remaining children think he/she was the favorite. Make sure siblings are told that they are important too.

Family arguments take on a new dimension. Each parent may feel that the other doesn't consider his/her suffering. When couples have been more parents than marriage partners, the stress of the loss of a child can cause the marriage to fail. Many marriages end after the death of a child. It drives people to examine their values, and if the marriage was shaky before the loss, it may seem no longer worth the effort.

Some parents feel that extended bereavement is a tribute to their child, and that years of grief symbolize the depth of their love. Having any joy brings a great deal of guilt.

Give yourself permission to have bad days without being panicked because you are backsliding. Equally, give yourself permission to have good days without being guilt-ridden because you still have moments of pleasure .

—Harriet Sarnoff Schiff

Loss of a stillborn or miscarried child

One form of loss that is often overlooked is loss of a child who was miscarried, stillborn, or who died soon after birth. The idea that there is no grief in the event is unfair to the mother and father. Failure by friends and family to recognize their loss leaves them isolated with their sorrow, unable to go through the normal grieving process afforded parents of a child who dies at the end of a short life. While parents of a young child who dies are treated with great sympathy, these parents' grief goes unacknowledged, as if no loss had occurred.

One father said, "Just because our son had not lived, it's as if he was never a human being." This attitude is heightened when parents' loss is brushed off with "you're young, you can always have another child." This fails to acknowledge that a baby has died—a loved and wanted child that both mother and father had felt move and in many cases, had seen however briefly, at birth.

Just as friends and family may avoid dealing with such a loss, parents who experience a stillbirth may react with denial, sometimes even refusing to view the baby's body. Many hospitals now work with parents experiencing high risk pregnancies. They have found that the most difficult problem a young couple has is coming to terms with the fact that the baby did actually exist and is now dead. Professionals have found that parents who leave the hospital without seeing the dead baby have the hardest time dealing with the reality of their loss.

When mothers and fathers of stillborn babies are given an opportunity to hold their babies, it is invariably the father who has the most difficulty letting it go.

There seems to be more sympathy in the case of miscarriage or stillbirth for the mother because she actually carried the baby. Some fathers feel that the mother is more fortunate because she had at least some contact with their child.

Answering a need

Some ways that hospitals are trying to address the very real resulting grief is by taking a picture of stillborn infants. The photograph is offered to the parents when the mother leaves the hospital, and if the photo is refused, it is kept on file. They also keep the child's identification bracelet if it lived even a few hours. They store these also because, more often than not, parents will want them at some later date.

Mental health practitioners trying to help couples come to grips with the loss of an infant often encourage them to name the baby to give it an identity and to show that he or she was a person who lived. Couples are encouraged to plan a funeral which makes friends and loved ones acknowledge the event and offer their condolences.

Parents who suffer miscarriage receive even less care and concern. Theirs is a loss of dreams and expectations. For those parents unable to conceive again, it is the death of hope. If they have no other children, the despair deepens. Understanding may come only from sharing their grief with others who have had a similar experience. For more information contact:

Bereaved Parents of the USA
P.O. Box 95
Park Forest, IL 60466
(708-748-7672)

Helping After Neonatal Death
P.O. Box 341
Los Gatos, CA 95031
http://www.h-a-n-d.org

Violent death

When a loved one has died violently, perhaps in a car crash, a victim of murder, a freak accident or suicide, there are many special issues that must be addressed. This is a death for which no one can be prepared. An anticipated death allows the opportunity to resolve feelings and relate lovingly during a loved one's final days, cushioning the impact of a final farewell.

In such cases, there are frightening and deeply unsettling thoughts and questions about that person's last minutes alive. Often the family becomes a subsequent victim at the hands of law officials who want information or even the press, which is forced into action by a public more and more eager for details.

It should bring some comfort to survivors to know that when people are seriously injured, they usually go into shock and do not feel pain. The fact of the death and how it occurred may be more painful to the survivors than to the victim. Ask questions. Accurate information about a death may allay unreasonable fears.

At such a traumatic time, let others take responsibilities. Confusion is a real part of multiple challenges to be faced after such an event.

Disenfranchised grief

When a loved one dies under socially sensitive conditions such as the result of suicide, AIDS, or as a crime victim, even those who would like to be supportive do not know how to respond. If there is enough ambivalence, the family may become isolated in their grief. Sometimes, as in the case of death due to AIDS, relatives may be just learning of their loved one's life style and may be coming to grips with that issue as well as his/her death. This has been termed disenfranchised grief, and in many cases both the family and those who would comfort them are confused as to what their response should be. It is doubly difficult to find words of sympathy without putting the bereaved in a position of having to explain embarrassing facts about the death. Any gesture of sympathy will let the family know that you are aware of their suffering.

In addition, much misinformation still remains about AIDS and the cause of it. It must never be assumed that just because someone died of AIDS or any disease for that matter that it is indicative of any particular lifestyle or way or life.

The unacknowledged mourners

Given the approximately two million deaths occurring in this country each year, the number of close friends and associates of these deceased persons is enormous. Although many friends become closer than "blood" relatives, the non-kin, non-spouse, friend, or colleague is seen as a passive mourner. They are largely ignored unless asked to offer eulogies or serve as pallbearers. Suggested means of grieving for a friend include:

- Write a note to the family with a specific anecdote about their loved one.
- Volunteer to be a "grief companion" to someone who has lost a friend.
- Continue a tradition initiated by a friend.
- Adopt one of your friend's good habits.
- Remember friends' family members.
- Make provisions in your will for gifts for friends.

Harold I. Smith, author of *Grieving the Death of a Friend*, notes that societal norms require that a friend's grief not compete with, overshadow, or complicate the family's grief. He believes, however, that "friend grief" should be validated and that it is both healthy and healing to keep pictures out as a reminder of that friendship. Smith recommends remembering the names of friends and even occasionally calling those names out loud, and when one wants to say, "_____ would have loved this," go ahead and say it—even if only to oneself.

Despite the passage of time and the absence of physical form, I feel their presence, their love, and their influence. The power of their lives is real, as when they were alive. They remain for me a tower of strength, a source of inspiration, and a constant influence for good work.
　　　　　—Alfred Kolatch, The Jewish Mourner's Book of Why

Specific loss

In some cases, a loss is so specific, whether as the result of death or associated with illness or other life situations, that persons seek the companionship of those suffering the same loss. *The Self-Help Sourcebook,* American Self-Help Clearinghouse, Attn: Sourcebook, St. Clares-Riverside Medical Center, Denville, NJ 07834 is an excellent resource. Updated every two years, the book is now in its fourth edition, and it contains over 600 national and model self-help groups. The book has proven helpful in creating community networks for forming self-help inter-groups. The information allows people to find or create the support group they need.

Support Groups

Recovery Inc.
802 N. Dearborn
Chicago, IL 60610

T.H.E.O.S (They Help Each Other Spiritually—widowed people)
322 Boulevard of the Allies, Suite 155
Pittsburg, PA 15222
(412) 471-7779

Compassionate Friends
P. O. Box 3696
Oak Brook, IL 60522
(630) 990-0010
http://www.compassionatefriends.org

Survivors Helping Survivor's (suicide)
St. Luke's Medical Center
2900 W. Oklahoma Ave.
Milwaukee, WI 53215

Victims of Crime Resource Center
McGeorge School of Law
University of the Pacific
3200 Fifth Ave.
Sacramento, CA 95817
800-Vic-tims

Center for Sibling Loss
The Southern School
1456 West Montose
Chicago, IL 60652

Parents of Murdered Children
100 E. 8th St., B-41
Cincinnati, OH 45202
(513) 721-LOVE

Penparents Inc.
P.O. Box 3737
Reno, NV 89507-8738
(702) 826-7332
http://www.penparents.com

Resources

Living Through Mourning: Finding Comfort and Hope When a Loved One Has Died, by Harriet Sarnoff Schiff
Seven Choices: Taking the Steps to New Life After Losing Someone You Love, by Elizabeth Harper Neeld, Ph.D.
Dimensions of Grief: Adjusting to the Death of a Spouse, by Stephen R. Shuchter
Beyond Widowhood, by Robert DiGiulio
Recovering From the Loss of a Child, by Katherine Fair Donnelly
After Suicide, by John H. Hewitt

When Pregnancy Fails: Families Coping with Miscarriage, Stillbirth, and Infant Death, by Susan Borg and Judith Lasker
Grieving the Death of a Friend, by Harold I. Smith

Death of a Pet

Over the past few years, another type of grief has been gaining acceptance—loss of a pet. People started domesticating animals some 12,000 years ago, and from that time on, interdependence between man and animal has increased. There is speculation that animals give humans signals about the natural world—the sight of roosting birds or sleeping dogs soothes because it signals the absence of danger.

One of the earliest known pet burials was found in northern Israel approximately 12,000 years ago. The excavated grave held skeletal remains of an elderly person and a young dog. The person's left hand rested on the animal in an eternal gesture of affection.

Today, 56% of households in the U.S. have dogs and cats (only 35% have children). For many owners, the presence of their pets has supported them through a number of life crises. Their pets have outlasted marriages, they've been there for their masters through serious illnesses, deaths of close family members, and other difficult times. They've been the single living being who has kept their owner from coming home to an empty house. Their loss is a real, deeply felt event. He/she may have been the last link to a special person or time in the owner's life—he "knew me when." When a pet dies, look for understanding from people who love animals—others will not comprehend the despair.

Adults often feel embarrassment and shame when they grieve deeply over the loss of a pet. In many cases a pet owner has lost a friend who gave unconditional love, and they have lost a life-style—greeting rituals, walks, a feeding regimen. Those who grieve for a pet go through many of the same feelings experienced when a human loved one is lost.

Euthanizing a pet

One form of death that is unique to pets is euthanasia, and, after this choice, there are special issues that may complicate the grieving process. Guilt is the most serious one (Should I have gotten a second opinion on the seriousness of my pet's illness? Was I too hasty—he could have had a few more days with me. I should have chosen to be with him when he died.).

Hard as it may seem at the time, pet owners feel better during mourning if they spend some quiet time with their pet for a final good-bye, whether they elect to be present during the actual procedure or not. For those who have not witnessed euthanasia, death is instantaneous and painless. When euthanasia is being considered, a pet owner should ask himself if refusing to make that choice would benefit the animal or himself. For a small extra cost, some veterinarians will euthenize the pet at the owner's home, making the event less traumatic for both the patient and its owner.

Helping pet owners cope

In 1980, the first full-time pet bereavement counselor was hired by the Veterinary Hospital of the University of Pennsylvania. Since that time, many animal hospitals have followed suit, and grief counselors for pet owners can be found in most cities by inquiring at animal care clinics.

Accidental death of a pet also carries added guilt because the animal's safety and well being depends almost entirely on the owner's judgement and care. The added weight of responsibility haunts the grieving owner with all the "if onlys" of imagined negligence.

When a pet dies, just as each family member has had a different relationship with the animal, each will experience a different kind of grief. Pets who start out belonging to the children often become the sole responsibility of a parent or grandparent. Because children are less self-conscious in showing their feelings, they often grieve and put their sorrow behind them more naturally than their elders. It is important that they be told that the pet has died rather than being given some fictitious account which leaves the child suffering a loss without the comfort that would ordinarily be offered. Discussing the death, though the child may not fully understand, and sharing your sorrow with him will set an example of natural reaction to death and may actually set the stage for dealing with greater losses that are bound to occur as he gets older.

Final arrangements

Just as the choice of final arrangements for loved ones can help people in the early stages of mourning their loss, so too can decisions about the final disposition of a pet. Several options are:

- **Private burials:** There are usually no restrictions for burial on residential property, though the veterinarian would be aware of local laws which may specify depths for the grave and types of containers for the body. Otherwise, a grave depth of three feet and use of a sealed container are recommended.
- **Private cremation:** Sometimes an animal shelter crematory offers only mass cremation. A veterinarian may be able to refer the pet owner to a crematory which will transport the body, perform an individual cremation for the pet, and deliver the ashes to the owner's home.
- **Animal hospital arrangements:** Veterinarians will offer to make arrangements to have the pet's body transported to a city-owned facility for mass cremation if the owner chooses.
- **Burial in a pet cemetery:** The vet can refer the owner to the nearest pet cemetery. Some cemeteries will transport the pet's body, provide a casket, burial plot, grave marker, floral arrangements, and other amenities.

Not only are the cemeteries good from a public health perspective . . . it's good from a public mental health perspective.

—*Susan Phillips Cohen*
Director of Manhattan's
Pet Loss Support Group

Today there are over 650 pet cemeteries in the United States, a number that has increased by about 10% per year over the past 15 years. The oldest is Hartsdale (New York) Canine Cemetery, which was established in 1896. This oldest pet cemetery is the site of a developing new trend of pet owner's burial beside their pets. Since pet burials are not allowed in human cemeteries, people have chosen Hartsdale in order to have their cremains buried near their pets. When pets survive their owners, they are now sometimes included in the owner's obituary.

Resources:

Pet Friends Inc.
Pet Loss Support Hotline
Moorestown, NJ
800-404-PETS

The Association for Pet Loss and Bereavement
P.O. Box 106
Brooklyn, NY 11230
(718) 382-0690
http://www.aplb.org

Books:
When A Pet Dies, by Fred Rogers (TV's Mr. Rogers)
When Your Pet Dies: How to Cope with Your Feelings, by Jamie Quackenbush, M. S. W. and Denise Graveline.

Chapter Ten

Helping the Young with Grief: Suffer the Little Children

Candice just turned five. She enjoys her visits with Grammie McGee. They bake cookies together, play dolls and Grammie always tells her stories about her own growing up. Grammie sings to Candice, and sometimes she lets her hold the China doll she played with when she was young. Now Candice is mad at her mother because she has come into her room crying and telling Candice that Grammie has gone to sleep and will never wake up again. Candice knows her mother is wrong—everyone who goes to sleep wakes up!

Children grieve differently from adults

Candice's mother meant well, but she didn't know how to speak to a child too young to understand the concept of death. In addition, euphemisms such as "gone to sleep and will never wake up" only add to the child's lack of comprehension and may cause fearfulness about sleeping. The concept of death can mean a variety of things depending on the age of the child, how close the child was to the deceased, and most importantly, how the child understands the permanence of death.

While recent research has shown that adults go through specific stages in the grief process, there is evidence that children grieve differently. Taking a child (especially a child over five-years-old) to a funeral of someone he was not close to (an acquaintance) can often make it much easier when a loved one dies because the child will then have an experience on which to base the information he is being given.

Talking about death

References to death and dying may be made relative to the age of the child, but euphemisms are seldom helpful at any age. Adults often use socially acceptable rhetoric such as "gone on," "passed away," or "left us." These abstract terms have little meaning for most children. Learn to use the words death and dying in such a context that children don't feel they are taboo or "unspeakable" subjects. Never diminish or belittle children when they ask or comment about death. This sends the message that their questions are insignificant or unimportant.

There is no "right time" to tell a child that someone has died. Research shows that psychologically a child copes much better when he hears the news from a family member rather than from a stranger. The most damaging thing that can be done is to send the child to visit someone until the entire funeral and death process is over. This not only makes the child feel disenfranchised from the family unit, it also does not allow for a sense of understanding of death, even if that understanding is rudimentary.

> Carousel
> By
> Ann Kinnaird
> I knew Grandfather was dead;
> I didn't have to be taken away
> from the family
> whispering on the porch
> under the wishing star.
> Hearing the muted song
> of the carousel that came
> to town that day
> one of the aunts
> said I'd be better off
> on a painted pony
> so she took my hand and
> walked me toward
> the lights.
> I knew what the grown-ups
> would do when I was gone:
> they would pass
> around Old Ezra
> to get ready for tomorrow.
> They could have done that
> with me there.
> Clinging to the brass
> pole lunging
> up and down,
> I looked at the swirling
> maze of bright
> lights and wished
> someone would talk to me
> about Grandfather.

Curiosity varies

Some children will be more curious than others about what happens to the body. Again, their understanding of this is a result of their age and maturity. Be factual and explain clearly and concisely what caused the death, "Grandma's heart stopped beating," or "Papaw fell and hit his head and hurt his brain." Explain that this is not common or necessarily going to happen to the child who might think that he/she might fall and die like his grandfather did.

Encourage communication regardless of the child's age. Assign words to your feelings whenever possible. "I'm sad today because it's Sunday, and I always liked visiting Aunt Mary on Sunday" or "Yes, there's a boat just like the one you and Grandpa used to go fishing in. Does that boat remind you of him?" Also remember that smells, sounds, and everyday items may remind the child of someone. Let the child express what he is feeling even if he doesn't know the right words.

Pre-school children

Because all children mature both emotionally and psychologically at different rates, it is important to remember that the following information, grouped by ages in general, is just a guideline. Children under three have no understanding of death, they do however, respond to the emotions of those around them. A child may perceive the sadness expressed by his parents without really understanding the cause. It is important that young children feel comfortable and have a sense of security while adults are going through the grieving process. Children under three learn by example, so when they see an adult who exhibits normal grief, they will soon learn it is not only natural, but healthy to cry and discuss feelings of loss.

Often the interruption of daily routines, as a result of a death in the family, is confusing for a child. Changes in sleeping and eating habits can result in a child who is irritable and cranky. In addition, a child may not receive the amount of attention normally shown to him. Parents need to be especially aware that their child may require more, not less, attention when someone close to the family dies.

In addition, parents must realize that non-compliant or acting-out behavior may be the result of disruption in daily routine and not a deliberate effort on the child's part to misbehave. Regression is common. Children potty trained for a long time may revert to bed-wetting after experiencing the death of someone close to them. A child who has slept in his own bed for years, even an older child, might try to get in bed with a parent, especially if the other parent has died.

Children under the age of six have little understanding of death as a permanent condition. According to Lillian Katz, a child development expert, pre-school age children don't see death as a continuing or irreversible condition. For the same reason, a child this age usually doesn't benefit from being able to say goodbye to someone who is terminally ill, while their school age peers do.

Time is a construct that very young children don't often grasp in the same sense that adults do, so it is very hard for them to really understand such abstracts as "forever." Permanence to a two-year-old is a concept that has no match in his world experience. In other words, when a child doesn't even understand the concept of a twenty-four hour day, how can he possibly understand forever? Some two and young three-year-old children don't even totally understand that when something is out of their sight it is not completely gone (object permanence), so they can hardly be expected to understand death. To them Grandma or Uncle Ned is always gone until he/she "reappears."

Just because a child seems to be aware of one death, he may not understand a similar one. How responsible that person was for the child's direct care will have more impact on a young child's reaction to death than a biological relationship. For example, a two year old may not seem to notice at all when her father dies, especially if he traveled frequently in his job and was only minimally involved with her care, whereas when an elderly babysitter dies, the child may become quite upset.

Children between the ages of four and six still see death as a temporary non-permanent condition. Since most children in this age group have been in childcare or daycare environments, they have come to understand that when Mom or Dad leaves in the morning to go to work, they always come back. For this reason, children in this age group (especially five and six-year-olds) might argue that Grandma or Grandpa is just "on a long trip and will too come back!" Children in this age group are still very sensitive to the emotional states of those around them, especially their parents and older siblings, so while they may actually cry and participate in the funeral process, it is not unusual for the grief to be forgotten quickly.

A child of three or four, is naturally curious about everything, so if he begins to ask questions about death, answer as completely as possible without saying, "you will understand in time." It is also common for a four or five year old child to ask the same question over and over in an abstract attempt to get another answer. A child who has lost a significant person such as a parent may regress to earlier behaviors such as biting, bed-wetting, or thumb-sucking in an attempt to cope with feelings they don't understand. Also children who have experienced the loss of a parent may seek attention from anyone, including strangers.

Four, five, and six-year-old children can and do learn to talk about their feelings, although they may not use adult words or phrases. In addition, children benefit from the freedom of being able to draw or color, even if they just scribble. By the time a child is five or six, depending on the family's religious orientation, he may begin to understand the concept of heaven or life after death. However, it is very important that children never are told that someone died because "God needed a new angel" or "Jesus needed Gramma in heaven with him." Children this age understand "need" only as it relates to them and their comfort. Therefore, a child might mistakenly blame God or the Higher Being for taking away something that the child needed.

Six to nine-year-olds

Six to nine-year-old children begin to really understand the permanence of death and can even be a big comfort during the grief process. Never force a child to attend a funeral or help with preparations for a "wake" or family gathering, but do allow them to participate if they are willing. It is common for a six or seven-year-old to ask questions which may seem insensitive to the adult such as, "Who will pick me up after school?" or "Where will we go in the summer if Grandpa is gone?" Never scold a child or diminish the importance of such questions as they are important to the child and certainly developmentally appropriate for a young child to ask. Children of this age may exhibit great understanding of the death of someone who was terminally ill, especially when they have observed or visited the person during the illness. It is common for a child to understand the death of an older person because they are beginning to understand the concept of aging and can see how living things grow old with time.

However, the same child who understood the death of a grandparent might have a particularly difficult time with the death of a pet and/or that of a young person. They feel helpless and may experience outbursts of anger. A six or seven year old may feel guilty or concerned that perhaps they in some way caused the death. This is not unlike what children experience when a divorce takes place during this time in their lives. Again, as with all children, the reaction to the death varies and is in a large way dependent on how the deceased person was perceived by the child. When a young child loses a parent, it is not uncommon for them to become very jealous and demanding of the remaining parent's time and attention.

Teachers often note that children in elementary school experience some belated feelings of helplessness, anxiety, sadness, and anger which show up several months or even a year after the death occurred. Play activities may become more aggressive as children act out "killing someone," or "killing something." A certain amount of this type of play is helpful as it allows the child to control aspects of his life which cannot otherwise be controlled. When children are killing a monster, it is quite possible they are acting out a hope that by "killing the imaginary monster" they can protect those they love. A child may have a series of bad dreams or nightmares which again are unconscious efforts to explain that over which he has no control.

Boys especially may constantly get into fights at school in an effort to express unnamed emotions which are a result of a death. Since stereotypically some young boys are still being told to "act like a man," "don't cry in front of others," and "keep a stiff upper lip," aggression toward others may be the only chance they have to express their anger and grief. It is very important that children this age be allowed to talk about what they are feeling. Art is a medium which allows them to express themselves. Whenever possible, children should be allowed to participate in a memorial or be allowed to talk about special times they shared with the loved one. As previously mentioned, always allow the child to cry, scream, or express himself/herself in any manner which seems right to the child.

As long as the child is not hurting himself or others physically, allow for some changes in behavior. Often children experience enormous guilt when someone dies, especially if it is a sibling. The child may feel guilty because he/she wished the sibling would "go away" so he could have more attention from mom or dad. The child may manifest a sense of guilt because of anger toward the deceased person or because he was left behind. Children who have survived when their sibling died may have latent feelings of unworthiness because they survived and their "more deserving" sibling didn't. In extreme cases, a child may appear distracted, become withdrawn or be unable to concentrate. This behavior may occur months after the death. One child became very distraught the first day of school and refused to ride the bus even though she had ridden it for the past four years. In her mind, because her favorite aunt had died in an accident involving a bus, she would too.

At daycare or school, teachers should not single out the grieving child in the classroom but should allow him an outlet (art, music) to express feelings. Asking a few of the child's friends to support him/her is often helpful in the elementary classroom. If a child becomes too angry or aggressive in play, it's important that the others in the class see that, while he must accept the consequences (removal from the play area) for such behavior, he may be acting out his grief or anger. Parents need to communicate with teachers and ask them to offer the child specific books to read or pair the child with another child who has been through a similar experience. How death is handled is a highly individual matter, and many families have very strong feelings about how they want their child to experience the process.

When talking about death, children may or may not cry. Even if you cry, they may not express themselves in that manner. Never ask a child why he/she didn't cry or respond in a certain way. Remember, adults and children cycle through the grief process quite differently. Never dictate to a child how she/he should feel, such as "Get over it, Andy died two years ago" or "Grow up, you've been sad long enough."

Ten to thirteen-year-olds

Ten to thirteen-year-old children tend to have a more adult understanding of the process of dying. They may be more reluctant to open up, but like three-year-olds, they can tune in to the feelings of those around them. However, unlike three-year-olds, ten to thirteen-year-olds will imitate the reactions of others. For this reason, the way adults in their presence grieve will very much determine how they outwardly express their grief.

Because early adolescence is such a volatile time, it is not uncommon for a pre-teen to try not to cry, to be overly concerned with what to wear to the funeral or even to express outbursts of anger when their social activities are disrupted by the death of a family member. After about age eight children begin to divide adults into three categories: handicapped, elderly (anyone over the age of 40) and young people. Therefore, a twelve year old might behave quite differently when a grandparent dies than when the teenage brother of an acquaintance dies.

To the adult, it seems that the child is behaving inappropriately by being more upset over the death of an acquaintance, but children this age often view themselves as indestructible or invincible. Therefore, they will have a more difficult time accepting the death of a casual acquaintance near their own age than that of an older relative.

Delayed reactions are common with older children. They may be able to respond quite well during the funeral and the period immediately after the death. In fact, parents have commented on how helpful their usually sullen teenager was during the preparation for the funeral, or how much their son helped with writing thank you notes when his father died, or how their daughter arranged flowers for her grandmother's funeral. However, six months later the same child is picked up for shop-lifting or sent home from school for fighting. While such extreme behavior is not without specific consequences, participating in a peer support group may help diminish destructive behavior resulting from the loss of someone close.

School performance may change or the preteen who slept eight hours every night may be caught watching television at three in the morning. Again, while these behaviors should never be dismissed because the child is grieving, helping the child express his or her feeling is very important. Support groups can be especially important — grieving children will often share things in a peer group that they would be reluctant to share with their own family. Avoid cliches such as, "Everything will be OK," "You sure are a big boy about this," or "You'll find another friend like the one you lost." This will alienate the preteen. Since independence is becoming a big issue for eleven to thirteen-year-olds, they will find such "babying" annoying and will respond negatively.

Spiritual aspects of death

Pre-adolescents and teens are naturally interested in spiritual aspects and may exhibit very strong feelings about the afterlife. The family's religious beliefs play an important role in how the older child perceives both life and death. However, some children might do things that seem to adults to be odd and out of sync with family values.

Thirteen year old Jake was raised in a traditional Christian family, yet when his grandfather died he went into the back yard and performed an Indian burial ritual he had read about in a book. While his parents found this behavior peculiar, it was appropriate for a boy curious about alternative belief systems.

Delayed mourning and holidays

Children may seem to accept the death of a loved one or friend until the first birthday or holiday celebrated without the person. If there were certain holiday rituals that the child experienced with the person who died, try to continue them if at all possible. If the child becomes upset or asks not to continue the practice, honor his wishes. Some children find comfort in the familiarity of "making Christmas cookies, just like Grandma did," while others may angrily respond, "You can't take the place of my daddy, he always cut up our turkey." During these times, a child may need to form new traditions or ways of dealing with the special occasion.

Amber's grandmother always gave her a doll for her birthday. The first birthday she had after her grandmother's death, her mother gave her a doll. To her mother's dismay, Amber took the doll and threw it on the floor. Rather than become angry, Amber's mother started a new tradition of giving her a stuffed animal rather than a doll.

One mother reported that her nine-year-old son wrote letters to his deceased grandfather for several years after his death, and the first Christmas, he insisted on buying his grandfather a present. This was hard for the mother, but later when she and her son read the letters together, he was able to accept the death. The following Christmas the family made a donation to a local charity in the grandfather's name, a tradition they have maintained for the past 15 years.

Years after a death, something might trigger a memory or a feeling that the child was unable to express at the time the death occurred. Allow the child to talk about it and, if possible, visit the grave or memorial site. Even if the child is unaware of what he is feeling, always let him know that you are there to listen and to validate what is going on in his/her mind. Remember, because a child was three or four when a sibling or parent died, they may be much older before they feel the full impact.

Teenagers and older adolescents

It often takes a teenager longer to begin to mourn. At first they may cope extremely well while adults facing the same loss are in the depths of grief. Then a second wave of pain and/or depression sets in, and the second round can be much harder to handle. Not only is it unexpected, it also seems grossly unfair. Often this is due to having blocked emotion in an effort to fend off pain. Some teenagers admit that once their stoicism subsides, their true feelings were allowed to surface. For some, this stage comes so long after the initial loss that memories have begun to fade, and the inability to recall their loved one creates anger.

To an adolescent, it often seems unreal and unbelievable that someone so necessary and important to them could actually die. The responses of denial, shock, and depression may serve to dampen overwhelming emotions enough that they can be tolerated.

"It seems like a bad dream."

"I can't believe I'll never see ___ again.
"I kept telling myself it won't happen." (expected death)

Shock is a normal defense against either physical or emotional trauma, or both, when a person is a bystander in an incident that involves the death of another. Shock insulates the body and mind by shutting both down, placing the person on "automatic pilot," buying time for adjustment to the new situation. People in shock sometimes behave in ways that seem inappropriate. Though they may appear perfectly normal, they may have no memory of their behavior afterward, and indeed may never remember their actions.

Adolescents experience pain, anger, guilt and regret just as adults do, but they often lack the maturity to examine their thoughts and feelings based on the reality of experience. There can be isolation in thinking they are the only ones who ever entertained such thoughts. Equally disturbing is the idea that they are crazy. Talking with a counselor or joining a support group with others who have been through the grieving process can help allay all these feelings. Learning that others are going through the same things can be comforting and reassuring.

Thoughts of suicide are also a part of grief, but when they become obsessive, they must be taken seriously. More and more American teenagers are committing suicide each year, and death of a parent, sibling, or significant friend can be devastating enough to cause great emotional upheaval. Sometimes a parent is too enmeshed in his/her own sorrow to notice the danger signs in an adolescent. In other cases, a young person may make it through one death only to face another a few months later and find the second loss too much to bear.

Returning to school

Returning to school after a death in the family is difficult. This may be the first public place in which the adolescent must handle his grief. Until then, he has been in the fairly protected environment of family and close friends. He may be overly conscious of how others expect him to act. All eyes may indeed be on him watching to see how he copes, less out of curiosity than in anticipation of having to respond and not knowing what to do or say to his classmate. Often this means a great void of silence both from the grieving student and his peers. On the other hand, schoolmates may come forward with a barrage of intimate and hurtful questions. Just a hug is probably the most appreciated response.

The empty desk—loss of a classmate

Perhaps because of the power of peer friendship, loss of a classmate or peer can be as disabling as loss of a parent or sibling. Depending on the strength of the relationship, not only is a companion lost, but a great source of support is gone at a time when it is most needed.

Loss of a popular classmate can cause a regrouping of friends. Occasionally friends will suddenly avoid the surviving best friend, perhaps feeling guilty that their primary friendships are still intact. Sometimes the absence of a particular personality will change the chemistry of a whole group, which may ultimately drift apart because of the sad changes.

With random violence occurring more often at school or school-related functions, there are sometimes multiple deaths with which fellow students must cope. This can be doubly stressful for those who either witnessed or were close by when friends' lives ended. At such times, proximity and later media attention can intensify feelings of anger, guilt, and pain, and efforts of special school counselors take on increased importance.

In all instances, teenagers find that having someone to talk with about their feelings is a great comfort. It is also a must in keeping them on track during the long healing process while surviving deep personal loss.

Sometimes, older teens may do volunteer work in memory of a loved one or may want to set up some type of shrine. Artistic teens enjoy making scrapbooks and creating works of art in memory of the person. Older children and adolescents appreciate and treasure being given something that belonged to the deceased. It need not be of great value to be meaningful.

On the night her grandfather died, Kimberly (14) asked for the watch he was wearing when he entered the hospital. Even though it was not one he wore often, she framed it and hung it by her bed.

Some adolescents may go through long periods of denial and act as if nothing every happened. Nancy was distraught when her husband Gary died, and their thirteen year old daughter went through the house taking down all his pictures. While this response may be viewed as lack of sensitivity by adults, in reality it is a natural form of coping that many experience. Eventually, the child should come to a place where he/she does want pictures or mementos of the person who died. If the child continues after nine to twelve months to act as if the person never lived at all, professional help may be warranted.

Support groups

There are many support groups and organizations dedicated to helping children and adults who assist them in coping with grief. In addition, many religious, civic and community organizations have grief support networks. Support groups for children and teenagers include:

Griefnet
P. O. Box 3272
Ann Arbor, MI 48106
http://www.griefnet.org

Compassionate Friends
P.O. Box 3696

Oak Brook, IL 605422
(630) 990-0010
http://www.compassionatefriends.org

Teenage Grief, Inc.
P.O. Box 220034
Newall, CA 91322-0034
661-253-1392
http://www.smartlink.net/~tag

Grieving is a process

Grieving is a process and, while the child will never stop remembering the person who died, in time, he will reach a point of acceptance. Daily life can be especially stressful for children who have lost someone close to them. A new friend may ask where his daddy is or how many sisters he has, and this may trigger those old feelings of guilt and fear. Children of any age require extra attention and understanding when they are grieving. It is wrong to assume that just because a child is young he/she will "get over" the loss. In reality, there is the hope that in time he will come to accept the loss.

Most importantly, model healthy emotional behavior for children. Allow them to laugh, cry, and talk about the deceased person. Just like adults, children of all ages need time and understanding in order to process the concept of death and dying.

Resources

Children and Grief: When a Parent Dies by J. William Worden.
Children Grieve Too: A Book for Families Who Have Experienced a Death by Joy and Marvin Johnson.
Children Mourning, Mourning Children by Kenneth Doka (editor), Hospice Foundation of America.
Healing the Bereaved Child by Alan D. Wolfelt.

How Do We Tell the Children: A Parents' Guide to Helping Children Understand & Cope When Someone Dies by Dan Schaefer and Christine Lyons.

The Grieving Child: A Parent's Guide by Helen Fitzgerald & Elizabeth Kubler-Ross.

On Children and Death by Elisabeth Kubler-Ross.

Teenagers Face to Face with Bereavement by Karen Gravelle and Charles Haskins.

Appendix

Appendix A State Insurance Commissions

Appendix B Organ Procurement Organizations

Appendix C Memorial Societies

Appendix D Veterans Affairs National Cemeteries

State Insurance Commissions

AK
Alaska Division of Insurance
Dept. of Commerce & Economic Dev.
P. O. Box 110805
Juneau, Alaska 99811-0805
907-465-2515
Fax: 907-465-3422

Federal Express Packages:
333 Willoughby Avenue, 9th Floor
Juneau, Alaska 99801

3601 C Street
Suite 1324
Anchorage, Alaska 99503-5948
907-269-7900
Fax: 907-269-7910

AL
Alabama Department of Insurance
201 Monroe Street, Suite 1700
Montgomery, Alabama 36104
334-269-3550
Fax: 334-241-4192

AR
Arkansas Department of Insurance
1200 West 3rd Street
Little Rock, Arkansas 72201-1904
501-371-2600
Fax: 501-371-2629

AS
Office of the Governor
American Samoa Government
Pago Pago, American Samoa 96799
011-684-633-4116
Fax: 011-684-633-2269

AZ
Arizona Department of Insurance
2910 North 44th Street, Suite 210
Phoenix, Arizona 85018-7256
602-912-8400
Fax: 602-912-8452

CA
California Department of Insurance
300 Capitol Mall, Suite 1500
Sacramento, California 95814
916-492-3500
Fax: 916-445-5280

State of California
45 Fremont Street, 23rd Floor
San Francisco, California 94102
415-538-4040
Fax: 415-904-5889

300 South Spring Street
Los Angeles, California 90013
213-346-6400
Fax: 213-897-6771

CO
Colorado Division of Insurance
1560 Broadway, Suite 850
Denver, Colorado 80202
303-894-7499
Fax: 303-894-7455

CT
Connecticut Department of Insurance
P.O. Box 816
Hartford, Connecticut 06142-0816

Federal Express Packages:
153 Market Street, 11th Floor
Hartford, Connecticut 06103
860-297-3802
Fax: 860-566-7410

DC
Dept. Of Insurance & Securities Reg.
Government of the District of Columbia
810 First Street, N. E.
Suite 701
Washington, DC 20002
202-727-8000 x3018
Fax: 202-535-1196

DE
Delaware Department of Insurance
Rodney Building
841 Silver Lake Boulevard
Dover, Delaware 19904
302-739-4251
Fax: 302-739-5280

FL
Florida Department of Insurance
State Capitol
Plaza Level Eleven
Tallahassee, Florida 32399-0300
850-922-3101
Fax: 850-488-3334

GA
Georgia Department of Insurance
2 Martin L. King, Jr. Dr.
Floyd Memorial Bldg., 704 West Tower
Atlanta, Georgia 30334
404-656-2056
Fax: 404-657-7493

GU
Dept. of Revenue & Taxation
Insurance Branch
Government of Guam
Building 13-3, 1st Floor
Mariner Avenue
Tiyan, Barrigada, Guam 96913

Post Office Box Address:
P.O. Box 23607
GMF, Guam 96921
671-475-1843
Fax: 671-472-2643

HI
Hawaii Insurance Division
Dept. of Commerce & Consumer Affairs
250 S. King Street, 5th Floor
Honolulu, Hawaii 96813

Post Office Box Address:
P.O. Box 3614
Honolulu, Hawaii 96811-3614
808-586-2790
Fax: 808-586-2806

IA
Division of Insurance
State of Iowa
330 E. Maple Street
Des Moines, Iowa 50319
515-281-5705
Fax: 515-281-3059

ID
Idaho Department of Insurance
700 West State Street, 3rd Floor
Boise, Idaho 83720-0043
208-334-4250
Fax: 208-334-4398

IL
Illinois Department of Insurance
320 West Washington St., 4th Floor
Springfield, Illinois 62767-0001
217-785-0116
Fax: 217-524-6500

100 West Randolph Street
Suite 15-100
Chicago, Illinois 60601-3251
312-814-2420
Fax: 312-814-5435

IN
Indiana Department of Insurance
311 W. Washington Street, Suite 300
Indianapolis, Indiana 46204-2787
317-232-2385
Fax: 317-232-5251

KS
Kansas Department of Insurance
420 S.W. 9th Street
Topeka, Kansas 66612-1678
785-296-7801
Fax: 785-296-2283

KY
Kentucky Department of Insurance
PO Box 517
215 West Main Street
Frankfort, Kentucky 40602-0517
502-564-6027
Fax: 502-564-1453

LA
Louisiana Department of Insurance
950 North 5th Street
Baton Rouge, Louisiana 70802

Post Office Box Address:
P.O. Box 94214
Baton Rouge, Louisiana 70804-9214
225-342-5423
Fax: 225-342-8622

MA
Division of Insurance
Commonwealth of Massachusetts
470 Atlantic Avenue, 6th floor
Boston, Massachusetts 02210-2223
617-521-7794
Fax: 617-521-7770

MD
Maryland Insurance Administration
525 St. Paul Place
Baltimore, Maryland 21202-2272
410-468-2090
Fax: 410-468-2020

ME
Maine Bureau of Insurance
Dept. of Professional & Financial Reg.
State Office Building, Station 34
Augusta, Maine 04333-0034

Federal Express Packages:
124 Northern Avenue
Gardiner, Maine 04345
207-624-8475
Fax: 207-624-8599

MI
Michigan Insurance Bureau
Department of Commerce
611 W. Ottawa Street, 2nd Floor North
Lansing, Michigan 48933-1020
517-373-9273
Fax: 517-335-4978

MN
Minnesota Department of Commerce
133 East 7th Street
St. Paul, Minnesota 55101
651-296-6848
Fax: 651-296-4328

MO
Missouri Department of Insurance
301 West High Street, 6 North
Jefferson City, Missouri 65102-690
573-751-4126
Fax: 573-751-1165

MS
Mississippi Insurance Department
1804 Walter Sillers
State Office Building
550 High Street
Jackson, MS 39201

Post Office Box Address:
P.O. Box 79
Jackson, MS 39205
601-359-3569
Fax: 601-359-2474

MT
Montana Department of Insurance
126 North Sanders
270 Mitchell Building
Helena, Montana 59601
406-444-2040
Fax: 406-444-3497

NC
North Carolina Department of Insurance
P.O. Box 26387
Raleigh, North Carolina 27611

Federal Express Packages:
Dobbs Building
430 N. Salisbury Street
Raleigh, North Carolina 27603
919-733-7349
Fax: 919-733-6495

ND
North Dakota Department of Insurance
600 E. Boulevard
Bismarck, North Dakota 58505-0320
701-328-2440
Fax: 701-328-4880

NE
Nebraska Department of Insurance
Terminal Building, Suite 400
941 'O' Street
Lincoln, Nebraska 68508
402-471-2201
Fax: 402-471-4610

NH
Department of Insurance
State of New Hampshire
56 Old Suncook Road
Concord, NH 03301
603-271-2261
Fax: 603-271-1406

NJ
New Jersey Department of Insurance
20 West State Street CN325
Trenton, New Jersey 08625
609-292-5360
Fax: 609-984-5273

NM
New Mexico Department of Insurance
P.O. Drawer 1269
Santa Fe, New Mexico 87504-1269

Federal Express Packages:
PERA Building
1120 Paseo de Peralta
Santa Fe, New Mexico 87501
505-827-4601
Fax: 505-476-0326

NV
Nevada Division of Insurance
1665 Hot Springs Road, Suite 152
Carson City, Nevada 89706-0661
775-687-4270
Fax: 775-687-3937

NY
New York Department of Insurance
25 Beaver Street
New York, New York 10004-2319
212-480-2289
Fax: 212-480-2310

Agency Building One
Empire State Plaza
Albany, New York 12257
518-474-6600
Fax: 518-473-6814

OH
Ohio Department of Insurance
2100 Stella Court
Columbus, Ohio 43215-1067
614-644-2658
Fax: 614-644-3743

OK
Oklahoma Department of Insurance
3814 N. Santa Fe
Oklahoma City, Oklahoma 73118
405-521-2828
Fax: 405-521-6635

OR
Oregon Division of Insurance
Dept. of Consumer & Business Services
350 Winter Street NE, Room 200
Salem, Oregon 97310-0700
503-947-7980
Fax: 503-378-4351

PA
Pennsylvania Insurance Department
1326 Strawberry Square, 13th Floor
Harrisburg, Pennsylvania 17120
717-783-0442
Fax: 717-772-1969

PR
Puerto Rico Dept. of Insurance
Cobian's Plaza Building
1607 Ponce de Leon Avenue
Santurce, Puerto Rico 00909

Post Office Box Address:
P.O. Box 8330
Fernandez Juncos Station
Santurce, Puerto Rico 00910-8330
787-722-8686
Fax: 787-722-4400

RI
Rhode Island Insurance Division
Dept. of Business Regulation
233 Richmond Street, Suite 233
Providence, Rhode Island 02903-4233
401-222-2223
Fax: 401-222-5475

SC
South Carolina Department of Insurance
1612 Marion Street
Columbia, South Carolina 29201

Post Office Box Address:
P.O. Box 100105
Columbia, South Carolina 29202-3105
803-737-6160
Fax: 803-737-6229

SD
South Dakota Division of Insurance
Dept. of Commerce & Regulation
118 West Capitol Avenue
Pierre, South Dakota 57501-2000
605-773-3563
Fax: 605-773-5369

TN
Tennessee Department of Commerce & Insurance
Volunteer Plaza
500 James Robertson Parkway
Nashville, Tennessee 37243-0565
615-741-2241
Fax: 615-532-6934

TX
Texas Department of Insurance
333 Guadalupe Street
Austin, Texas 78701

Post Office Box Address:
P.O. Box 149104
Austin, Texas 78714-9104
512-463-6464
Fax: 512-475-2005

UT
Utah Department of Insurance
3110 State Office Building
Salt Lake City, Utah 84114-1201
801-538-3800
Fax: 801-538-3829

VA
State Corporation Commission
Bureau of Insurance
Commonwealth of Virginia
P.O. Box 1157
Richmond , Virginia 23218

Federal Express packages:
Virginia Bureau of Insurance
State Corporation Commission
1300 East Main Street
Richmond, Virginia 23219
804-371-9694
Fax: 804-371-9873

VI
#18 Kongens Gade Charlotte Amalie
St. Thomas, Virgin Islands 00802
340-774-7166
Fax: 340-774-9458 or 340-774-6953

Division of Banking & Insurance
1131 King Street, Suite 101
Christiansted
St. Croix, Virgin Islands 00820
340-773-6449
Fax: 340-773-4052

VT
Vermont Division of Insurance
Dept. of Banking, Insurance & Securities
89 Main Street, Drawer 20
Montpelier, Vermont 05620-3101
802-828-3301
Fax: 802-828-3306

WA
Washington Office of the Insurance Commissioner
14th Avenue & Water Streets
P.O. Box 40255
Olympia, Washington 98504-0255
360-753-7301
Fax: 360-586-3535

WI
Office of the Commissioner of Insurance
State of Wisconsin
121 E. Wilson
Madison, Wisconsin 53702

Post Office Address
P.O. Box 7873
Madison, Wisconsin 53707-7873
608-267-1233
Fax: 608-261-8579

WV
West Virginia Department of Insurance
P.O. Box 50540
Charleston, West Virginia 25305-0540

Federal Express Packages:
State of West Virginia
1124 Smith Street
Charleston, West Virginia 25301
304-558-3354

WY
Wyoming Department of Insurance
Herschler Building
122 West 25th Street, 3rd East
Cheyenne, Wyoming 82002-0440
307-777-7401
Fax: 307-777-5895

NAIC Headquarters
120 W. 12th Street
Suite 1100
Kansas City, Missouri 64105-1925
816-842-3600
Fax: 816-471-7004

Organ Procurement Organizations

AL
ATTN: Public Relations
Alabama Organ Center
619 South 19th Street
Birmingham, AL 35233

AR
ATTN: Public Relations
Arkansas Regional Organ Recovery Agency
1100 N. University, Suite 200
Little Rock, AR 72207

AZ
ATTN: Public Relations
Donor Network of Arizona
3877 North 7th St., Suite 200
Phoenix, AZ 85014

CA
ATTN: Public Relations
Southern CA Organ Procurement Ctr.
2100 W. Third St., Suite 350
Los Angeles, CA 90057

ATTN: Public Relations
California Transplant Donor Network
55 Francisco St. Suite 510
San Francisco, CA 94133

ATTN: Public Relations
Organ & Tissue Acquisition Ctr. of Southern CA
3500 Fifth Ave., Suite 203
San Diego, CA 92103

ATTN: Public Relations
Regional Organ Pro. Agcy. of Southern CA
10920 Wilshire Blvd., Suite 910
Los Angeles, CA 90024-6511

ATTN: Public Relations
Golden State Transplant Services
1760 Creekside Oaks Dr., Suite 160
Sacramento, CA 95833

CT
ATTN: Public Relations
Hartford Organ Procurement Organization
Hartford Hospital
P. O. Box 5037
Hartford, CT 06102-5037

CO
ATTN: Public Relations
Colorado Organ Recovery Systems, Inc.
3773 Cherry Creek North Dr., Suite 601
Denver, CO 80209

FL
ATTN: Public Relations
University of Miami Organ Procurement
1600 NW 10th Ave.
Miami, FL 33136

ATTN: Public Relations
TRANSLIFE
2501 N. Orange Ave., Suite 40
Orlando, FL 32804

ATTN: Public Relations
OPO of the University of Florida
P. O. Box 100286
Gainesville, FL 32610

ATTN: Public Relations
Lifelink of Florida, Inc.
2111 West Swann Avenue
Tampa, FL 33606-2486

GA
ATTN: Public Relations
Lifelink of Georgia
3715 Northside Parkway
100 North Creek, Suite 300
Atlanta, GA 30327

ATTN: Public Relations
Medical College of Georgia
Organ & Tissue Donor Services
BA-A232,1120 15th St.
Augusta, GA 30912-4097

HI
ATTN:Public Relations
Organ Donor Center of Hawaii
1000 Bishop St., Suite 302
Honolulu, HI 96813

IA
ATTN: Public Relations
Iowa Statewide OPO
328 Westlawn
Iowa City, IA 52242

IL
ATTN: Public Relations
Regional Bank of Illinois
800 S. Wells, Suite 190
Chicago, IL 60607

IN
ATTN: Public Relations
Indiana Organ Procurement Organization, Inc.
719 Indiana Ave., Suite 100
Indianapolis, IN 46202

KS
ATTN:Public Relations
Midwest Organ Bank, Inc.
1000 W. 47th Place, Suite 400
Westwood, KS 66205

KY
ATTN: Public Relations
Kentucky Organ Donor Affiliates
305 W. Broadway, Suite 316
Louisville, KY 40202

LA
ATTN: Public Relations
Louisiana Organ Procurement Agency
3501 N. Causeway Blvd., Suite 940
Metairie, LA 70002-3626

MA
ATTN: Public Relations
New England Organ Bank
One Gateway Center
Washington St. at Newton Corner
Newton, MA, 02158-2803

MD
ATTN: Public Relations
Transplant Resource Center of Maryland
1540 Caton Center Dr., Suite R
Baltimore, MD 21227

MI
ATTN: Public Relations
Organ Procurement Agency of Michigan
2203 Plaft Road
Ann Arbor, MI 48104

MO
ATTN: Public Relations
Mid-America Transplant Association
1139 Olivette Executive Parkway
St. Louis, MO 63132

MS
ATTN: Public Relations
Mississippi Organ Recovery Agency
826R Lakeland Drive, Suite 200
Jackson, MS 39216

MN
ATTN: Public Relations
LifeSource, Upper Midwest Organ Procure.
3433 Broadway St., N.E., Suite 260
Minneapolis, MN 55413

NC
ATTN: Public Relations
LifeShare of the Carolinas
I. P. 0. Box 32861
Charlotte, NC 28232-2861

ATTN: Public Relations
Carolina Organ Procurement Agency
702 Johns Hopkins Drive
Greeneville, NC 27834

ATTN: Public Relations
Carolina LifeCare
Medical Center Boulevard
Winston-Salem, NC 27157

NE
ATTN: Public Relations
Nebraska Organ Retrieval System, Inc.
4060 Vinton Street, Suite 200
Omaha, NE 68105

NJ
ATTN: Public Relations
New Jersey Organ & Tissue Sharing Network
150 Morris Avenue
Springfield, NJ 07081

NM
ATTN: Public Relations
New Mexico Donor Program
2715 Broadbent Parkway, Suite J
Albuquerque, NM 87107

NV
ATTN: Public Relations
Nevada Donor Network, Inc.
4580 S. Eastern Ave., Suite 33
Las Vegas, NV 89119-6105

NY
ATTN: Public Relations
OPO of Albany Medical College
47 New Scotland Ave., A-98
Albany, NY 12208

ATTN: Public Relations
Upstate New York Transplant Service, Inc.
1093 Delaware Ave.
Buffalo, NY 14209

ATTN: Public Relations
New York Regional Transplant Program, Inc.
475 Riverside Dr., Suite 1244
New York, NY 10115-1244

ATTN: Public Relations
Long Island Transplant Program
University Hospital of SUNY-Stony Brook
Health Sciences Center
Stony Brook, NY 11794-8192

ATTN: Public Relations
University of Rochester, OPO
1458 Chili Avenue
Rochester, NY 14624

OH
ATTN: Public Relations
Life Connection of Ohio
1545 Holland Road, Suite C
Maumee, OH 43537-1694

ATTN: Public Relations
Lifeline of Ohio Organ Procurement Agcy., Inc.
700 Ackerman Rd., Suite 580
Columbus, OH 43202

ATTN: Public Relations
Life Bank
20600 Chagrin Blvd., Suite 350
Cleveland, OH 44122-5343

ATTN: Public Relations
Ohio Valley Life Center
2939 Vernon Place
Cincinnati, OH 45219

OK
ATTN: Public Relations
Oklahoma Organ Sharing Network
5801 North Broadway, Suite 100
Oklahoma City, OK 73118

OR
ATTN: Public Relations
Pacific NW Transplant Bank
2611 SW 3rd Ave., Suite 320
Portland, OR 97201-4952

SC
ATTN: Public Relations
South Carolina Organ Procurement Agency, Inc.
1064 Gardner Rd., Suite 105
Charleston, SC 29407

PA
ATTN: Public Relations
CORE
204 Sigma Drive
Pittsburgh, PA 15238-2825

ATTN: Public Relations
Delaware Valley Transplant Program
Rodin Place, Suite 201
2000 Hamilton Street
Philadelphia, PA 19130-3813

TN
ATTN: Public Relations
Mid-South Transplant Foundation, Inc.
956 Court Ave., Suite G-228
Memphis, TN 38163

ATTN: Public Relations
Life Resources Regional Donor Center
2812 McKinley Road
Johnson City, TN 37604

ATTN: Public Relations
Tenessee Donor Services
1714 Hayes Street
Nashville, TN 37208

TX
ATTN: Public Relations
LifeGift Organ Donation Center
5615 Kirby Drive, Suite 900
Houston, TX 77005

ATTN: Public Relations
Southwest Organ Bank, Inc.
3500 Maple Ave., Suite 800
Dallas, TX 75219

ATTN: Public Relations
South Texas Organ Bank, Inc.
8122 Datapoint Dr., Suite 1150
San Antonio, TX 78229

UT
ATTN: Public Relations
Intermountain Organ Recovery Systems
230 South 500 East, Suite 290
Salt Lake City, UT 84102

VA
ATTN: Public Relations
LifeNet Transplant Services
5809 Ward Court
Virginia Beach, VA 23455

ATTN: Public Relations

Washington Regional Transplant Consortium
8110 Gatehouse Rd., Suite 101-West
Falls Church, VA 22042

WA
ATTN: Public Relations
Sacred Heart Organ Procurement Agency
P. 0. Box 2555
Spokane, WA 99220-2555

ATTN: Public Relations
Northwest Organ Procurement Agency
600 Broadway, Suite 260
Seattle, WA 98122

WI
ATTN: Public Relations
Wisconsin Donor Network
9200 W. Wisconsin Ave.
Milwaukee, WI 53226

ATTN: Public Relations
University of Wisconsin, OPO
600 Highland Ave.
Madison, WI 53792

Memorial Societies

Continental Association of
Funeral and Memorial Societies, Inc.
6900 Lost Lake Road, Egg Harbour, WI 54209.
Fax/Tel: 414-868-3136

AK
Cook Inlet Memorial Society
P.O. Box 102414,
Anchorage, AK 99510
907-563-7507

AR
Northwest Arkansas Memorial Society
P.O. Box 3055
Fayetteville, AR 72702-3055
501-443-1404

AZ
Mesa Valley Memorial Society
Box 31545,
Mesa Valley, AZ 85275-1545
602-807-5155

Memorial Society of Prescott
335 E. Aubrey St.,
Prescott, AZ 86303
602-778-3000

Tucson Memorial Society
P.O. Box 12661,
Tucson, AZ 85732-2661
602-721-0230

Memorial Society of Yuma
Box 4314
Yuma, AZ 85366-4314
602-726-8014

CA
Kern Memorial Society
P.O. Box 1202,
Bakersfield, CA 93302-1202
805-366-7266 or 805-854-5689

Bay Area Funeral Society
P.O. Box 264,
Berkeley, CA 94701-0264
510-841-6653

Redwood Funeral Society
P.O. Box 7501,
Cotati, CA 94931-7501
707-829-0848

Eureka Humboldt Funeral Society
P.O. Box 2716,
McKinleyville, CA 9521-2716
707-822-2445

Santa Cruz Funeral and M. S. of Monterrey Bay
Box 2900
Santa Cruz, CA 95063-2900
408-426-1333

Fresno Valley Memorial Society
P.O. Box 101,
Fresno, CA 93707-0101
209-268-2181

Los Angeles Funeral Society
P.O. Box 92313
Pasadena, CA 91109-2313
818-791-4829

Stanislaus Memorial Society
P.O. Box 4252
Modesto, CA 95352-4252
209-521-7690

Peninsula Memorial Society
P.O. Box 60448
Palo Alto, CA 94306-0448
415-321-2109

Sacramento Valley Mem. Society
P.O. Box 161688,
Sacramento, CA 95816-1688
916-451-4641

San Diego Memorial Society
P.O.Box 16336,
San Diego, CA 92176-6336
619-293-0926

Ventura Channel Cities Memorial Society
4101 E. Hampden Ave.,
Ventura, CA 80222
303-759-2800

CT
Mem. Soc. of Southwest Connecticut
71 Hillendale Rd.
Westport, CT 06880
203-227-8705

FL
Cocoa Funeral and M.S. of Brevard County
P.O. Box 276,
Cocoa Beach, FL 32923-0276
407-453-4109 or 407-636-3363

San Joaquin Memorial Society
Box 4832
Stockton, FL , 95204-4832
209-466-7743

Funeral Society of Mid Florida
P.O. Box 4478,
Deland, FL 32723-4478
904-789-1682 or 904-734-9280

Ft. Myers Funeral and M.S. of Southwest Florida
P.O. Box 7756
Fort Myers, FL 33911-7756
813-939-3368

Mem. Soc. Of Northwest Florida
P.O. Box 4122
Fort Walton Beach, FL 32549-4122
904-862-6706

Mem. Soc. Of Alachua County
Box 14662
Gainsville, FL 32604-4662
904-332-5834

Miami Memorial Society
3420 Segovia
Miami, FL 33134
305-461-1251

Mem. & Funeral Soc., of Greater Orlando
P.O. Box 953,
Goldenrod, FL 32733-0953
407-677-5009

Funeral & Memorial Society of Pensacola & West Florida
7804 Northpointe Blvd.
Pensacola, FL 32514
904-932-9566 or 904-477-8431

Memorial Society of Sarasota
P.O. Box 15833
Sarasota, FL 34277-5833
813-953-3740

Suncoast-Tampa Bay Mem. Society
719 Arlington Ave. N.,
St. Petersburg, FL 33701
813-898-3294

Funeral and Mem. Soc. of Leon County
1006 Buena Vista Dr.
Tallahassee, FL 32304
904-224-2082

Tampa Memorial Society
3915 North AAA St.
Tampa, FL 33609
813-877-4604

Palm Beach Funeral Society
P.O. Box 2065
West Palm Beach, FL 33402-2065
407-833-8936

GA
Memorial Society of Georgia
1911 Cliff Valley Way NE
Atlanta, GA 30329
404-634-2896

HI
Memorial Society of Hawaii
2510 Bingham St., Rm. A
Honolulu, HI 96826
808-946-6822

ID
Boise Idaho Memorial Association
P.O. Box 1919
Boise, ID 83701-1919
208-343-4581

IL
Chicago Memorial Association
Box 2923
Chicago, IL 60690-2923
312-939-0678

Champaign County Memorial Society
309 W. Green St.
Urbana, IL 61801
217-384-8862

IN
Bloomington Memorial Society
2120 N. Fee Lane
Bloomington, IN 47408
812-332-3695

Memorial Society of Northeast Indiana
2215 California,
Ft. Wayne, IN 46805
219-484-0109

Indianapolis Memorial Society
5805 E. 56th St.
Indianapolis, IN 46226
317-844-1371 or 317-545-6005

Memorial Society of Northwest Indiana
356 McIntyre Court
Valparaiso, IN 46383
219-462-5701

IA
Memorial Society of Central Iowa
2020 Pinehurst
Ames, IA 50010
515-292-5960

Funeral and Memorial Society of Iowa
2233 W 13th St.
Davenport, IA 52804
319-322-3400

Memorial Society of Iowa River Valley
120 N. Dubuque St.
Iowa City, IA 52245
319-338-2637

KY
Memorial Society of Central Kentucky
3564 Clays Mill Rd.
Lexington, KY 40503
606-223-1448

Memorial Society of Greater Louisville
891 Minoma Ave.
Louisville, KY 40217
502-637-5911

LA
Mem. Soc. of Greater Baton Rouge
8470 Goodwood Ave.
Baton Rouge, LA 70806
504-926-2291

MA
Memorial Society of Cape Cod
45 Foster Road
Brewster, MA 02631
617-896-3370

Memorial Society of Greater Brockton
325 W. Elm St.
Brockton, MA 02401
508-238-6373

Memorial Society of Massachusetts Bay
66 Marlborough St.
Boston, MA 02116
617-859-7990

Memorial Soc. of S. E. Massachusetts
71 8th St.
New Bedford, MA 02740
508-994-9686 or 508-679-6835

Springfield Memorial Society
P.O. Box 2821
Springfield, MA 01101-2821
413-783-7987

MD
Bethesda Memorial Society of Maryland
9601 Cedar Lane
Bethesda, MD 20814
301-564-0006

ME
Memorial Society of Maine
Box 3122
Auburn, ME 04212-3122
207-786-4323

MI
Ann Arbor Memorial Advisory and Planning Service
2030 Chaucer Drive
Ann Arbor, MI 48103
313-665-9516

Greater Detroit Memorial Society
P.O. Box 24054
Detroit, MI 48224-4054
313-886-0998

Memorial Society of Flint
P.O. Box 4315
Flint, MI 48504-4315
313-239-2596

Lansing Area Memorial Planning Society
765 Collingwood
East Lansing, MI 48823
517-351-3980

MN
Minnesota Funeral and Mem. Soc.
717 Riverside Dr. SE
St. Cloud, MN 56304
612-252-7540

MO
Greater Kansas City Memorial Society
4500 Warwick Blvd.
Kansas City, MO 64111
816-561-6322

St. Louis Memorial and Planned Funeral Society
5007 Waterman Blvd.
St. Louis, MO 63108
314-361-0595

MT
Memorial Society of Montana
1024 Princeton Ave.
Billings, MT 59102
406-252-5065

Five Valleys Burial Memorial Association
405 University Ave.
Missoula, MT 59801
406-543-6952

NC
Blue Ridge Memorial Society
P.O. Box 2601
Ashville, NC 28802-2601
704-669-2587

Triangle Memorial and Funeral Society
P.O. Box 1223
Chapel Hill, NC 27514-1223
919-942-4994

Greensboro Piedmont Memorial & Funeral Society
5137 Charleston Rd.
Pleasant Garden, NC 27313
919-674-5501

Scotland County Funeral & Memorial Soc.
P.O. Box 192
Laurinburg, NC 28352-0192
919-276-6536

Mem. Soc. of Lower Cape Fear
P.O. Box 4262
Wilmington, NC 28406-4262
919-392-6454

NV
Memorial Society of Western Nevada
Box 8413 University Station
Reno, NV 89507-8413
702-852-4600

NH
Memorial Society of New Hampshire
P.O. Box 941
Epping, NH 03042-0941
603-679-5721

NJ
Memorial Society of South New Jersey
401 Kings Highway N.
Cherry Hill, NJ 08034
609-667-3618

Raritan Valley Memorial Society
176 Tice's Lane
East Brunswick, NJ 08816
908-246-3113

Memorial Association of Monmouth County
1475 W. Front St.
Lincroft, NJ 07738
908-747-0707

Morris Memorial Society
Box 509
Madison, NJ 07940-0509
201-540-9140

Paramus Central Memorial Society
156 Forest Ave.
Paramus, NJ 07652
201-836-7267

Memorial Society of Plainfield
858 Princeton Ct.,Neshanic Sta
Plainfield, NJ 08853-9686
908-369-7260

Princeton Memorial Association
48 Roper Road
Princeton, NJ 08540
609-924-5525

Memorial Society of Essex
P.O. Box 888
Upper Montclair, NJ 07043-0888
201-783-1145

NM
Memorial & Funeral Soc. of So. New Mexico
P.O. Box 6531
Las Cruces, NM 88006-6531
505-522-3335

NY
Memorial. Soc. of the Hudson-Mohawk Region
405 Washington Ave.
Albany, NY 12206-2604
518-465-9664

Southern Tier Memorial Society
183 Riverside Dr.
Binghamton , NY 13905
607-729-1641

Greater Buffalo Memorial Society
695 Elmwood Ave.
Buffalo, NY 14222-1601
716-885-2136

Memorial Society of Greater Corning Area
P.O. Box 23, Painted Post
Corning, NY 14870-0023
607-962-7132

Memorial Soc. of Long Island
Box 3495
Farmington, NY 11735-0694
516-627-6590

Hormell Upper Genesee Memorial Society
33 S. Main St.
Alfred, NY 14802
607-587-8429

Ithaca Memorial Society
Box 134
Ithaca, NY 14851-0134
607-273-8316

Mohawk Valley Memorial Society
P.O. Box 322
New Hartford, NY 13413-0322
315-735-6268

Memorial Society of Riverside Church
490 Riverside Drive,
New York, NY 10027
212-222-5900

Community Church of NY Funeral Soc.
40 East 35th St.
New York, NY 10016
212-683-4988

Rockland County Memorial Society
Box 461
Pamona, NY 10970-0461
914-354-1789

Mid-Hudson Memorial Society
249 Hooker Ave.
Poughkeepsie, NY 12603
914-229-0241

Rochester Memorial Society
220 Winton Road
South Rochester, NY 14610
716-461-1620

Syracuse Memorial Society
P.O. Box 67
DeWitt , NY 13214-0067
315-478-7258

Memorial Society of Northern NY
1138 Harrison St.
Watertown, NY 13601
315-782-4999

Westchester Funeral Planning Association
Rosedale Ave. & Sycamore Ln.
White Plains, NY 10605
914-946-1660

OH
Memorial Society of Akron-Canton Area
3300 Morewood Road
Akron, OH 44333
216-836-2206

Memorial Society of Greater Cincinnati
536 Linton St.
Cincinnati. OH 45219
513-281-1564

Cleveland Memorial Society
21600 Shaker Blvd.
Shaker Heights, OH 44122
216-751-5515

Memorial Society of the Columbus Area
P.O. Box 14835
Columbus, OH 43214-4835
614-436-8911

Dayton Memorial Society
665 Salem Ave.
Dayton, OH 45406
513-274-5890

Memorial Society of Northwest Ohio
2210 Collingwood Blvd.
Toledo, OH 43620-1147
419-475-1429

Waverly Branch of Mem. Soc. of Columbus Area
111 Wendy Lane
Columbus, OH 45690
614-947-2118

Yellow Springs Branch of Mem. Soc. of Columbus Area
317 Dayton St.
Columbus, OH 45387
513-767-1659

Memorial. Society of Greater Youngstown
1702 Beechwood Ave. N.E.
Warren, OH 44483
216-372-5267

OR
Emerald Memorial Association
P.O. Box 11347
Eugene, OR 97440-3547
503-345-0639

Portland Oregon Memorial Association
811 E. Burnside,
Suite 122,
Portland, OR 97214-1231
503-239-0150

PA
Lehigh Valley Memorial Society
2502 Washington St.
Allentown, PA 18104
215-820-5004

Memorial Society of Erie
Box 3495
Erie, PA 16508-3495
814-864-9300

Memorial Society of Greater Harrisburg
1280 Clover Lane
Harrisburg, PA 17113
717-564-4761

Memorial Soc. of Greater Philadelphia
2125 Chestnut St.
Philadelphia, PA 19103
215-567-1065

Pittsburgh Memorial Society
605 Morewood Ave.
Pittsburg, PA 15213
412-612-4740

Memorial Soc. of Central Pennsylvania
780 Waupelani Dr. Ext.
State College, PA 16801
814-237-7605

RI
Mem. Soc. of Rhode Island
119 Kenyon Ave.
East Greenwich, RI 02818
401-884-5933

TN
Memorial Society of Chattanooga
3224 Navajo Dr.
Chattanooga, TN 37411
615-899-9315

Knoxville-East Tennessee Memorial Society
111 Columbia Drive
Oak Ridge, TN 37830
615-483-4843

Middle Tennessee Memorial Society
1808 Woodmont Blvd.
Nashville, TN 37215
615-383-5760

TX
Austin Memorial. & Burial Information Society
P.O. Box 4382
Austin, TX 78765-4382
512-836-8104

Memorial Society of North Texas
4015 Normandy
Dallas, TX 75205
214-528-6006

Denton Memorial Society of North Texas
4015 Normandy,
Dallas, TX 75205
800-371-2221

Memorial Society of El Paso
P.O. Box 4951
El Paso, TX 79914-4951
505-824-4565

Memorial Society of North Texas
1959 Sandy Lane,
Fort Worth, TX 76112
800-371-2221

Houston Area Memorial Society
5200 Fannin St.
Houston, TX 77004-5899
713-526-4267

Lubbock Area Memorial Society
Box 6562
Lubbock, TX 79413-6562
214-528-6006

San Antonio Memorial Society
7150 Interstate 10 West
San Antonio, TX 78213
210-341-2213

Wichita Falls Memorial Society of North Texas
4015 Normandy
Dallas, TX 75205
800-371-2221

UT
Utah Memorial Association
307 M Street
Salt Lake City, UT 84103
801-581-6608

VA
Mt. Vernon Memorial Society
1909 Windmill Lane
Alexandria, VA 22307
703-765-5950

Memorial Society of Northern Virginia
4444 Arlington Blvd.
Arlington, VA 22204
703-271-9240

Memorial Planning Soc. of the Piedmont
717 Rugby Road
Charlottesville, VA 22903
804-293-8179

Memorial. Soc. of Greater Richmond Area
P.O. Box 29315
Richmond, VA 23229-9315
804-285-9157

Memorial Society of Tidewater
P.O. Box 4621,
Virginia Beach, VA 23454-4621
804-481-2991

VT
Vermont Memorial Society
Box 67
Burlington, VT 05401-0067
802-862-7474

WA
People's Memorial Association
2366 Eastlake Ave. E., #409
Seattle, WA 98102
206-325-0489

Spokane Memorial Association
P.O. Box 13613
Spokane, WA 99213-13613
509-924-8400

Funeral Assoc. of Central Washington
P.O. Box 379
Yakima, WA 98907-0379
509-452-1712

WI
Memorial Society of Door County
6900 Lost Lake Rd.
Egg Harbor, WI 54209-9231
414-868-3136

Memorial Society of Madison
5235 Harbor Court
Madison, WI 53705
608-255-8333

Funeral and Memorial Society of Greater Milwaukee
13001 W. North Ave.
Brookfield, WI 53005
414-782-3535

Racine Memorial Society of Southeast Wisconsin
(Temp) 6900 Lost Lake Rd.,
Egg Harbor, WI 54209
414-552-8540

WV (Served by Maryland Memorial Society)

Veterans Affairs National Cemeteries

The U.S. Department of Veterans Affairs (VA) National Cemetery Administration maintains 115 national cemeteries in 39 states (and Puerto Rico) as well as 33 soldier's lots and monument sites.
The following is a list of addresses and phone numbers of VA National Cemeteries . Please note that there is not a VA national cemetery in every state. You may also want to check the listing of State veterans cemeteries.

AL
Fort Mitchell National Cemetery
553 Highway 165
Seale, AL 36875
(334) 855-4731

Mobile National Cemetery
1202 Virginia Street
Mobile, AL 36604
For information please contact: Barracas National Cemetery
(850) 452-3357

AK
Fort Richardson National Cemetery
Building #997, Davis Highway
P. O. Box 5-498
Fort Richardson, AK 99505
(907) 384-7075

Sitka National Cemetery
Box 1065
Sitka, AK 99835
For information please contact: Fort Richardson National Cemetery (907) 384-7075

AR
Fayetteville National Cemetery
700 Government Avenue
Fayetteville, AR 72701
(501) 444-5051

Fort Smith National Cemetery
522 Garland Avenue
Fort Smith, AR 72901
(501) 783-5345

Little Rock National Cemetery
2523 Confederate Boulevard
Little Rock, AR 72206
(501) 324-6401

AZ
National Memorial Cemetery of Arizona
23029 North Cave Creek Road
Phoenix, AZ 85024
(602) 379-4615P

Prescott National Cemetery
VA Medical Center
500 Highway 89 North
Prescott, AZ 86301
For information please contact: National Memorial Cem. of Arizona (602) 379-4615

CA
Fort Rosecrans National Cemetery
P. O. Box 6237 Point Loma
San Diego, CA 92106
(619) 553-2084

Golden Gate National Cemetery
1300 Sneath Lane
San Bruno, CA 94066
(415) 761-1646

Los Angeles National Cemetery
950 South Sepulveda Boulevard
Los Angeles, CA 90049
(310) 268-4675

Riverside National Cemetery
22495 Van Buren Boulevard
Riverside, CA 92518
(909) 653-8417

San Francisco National Cemetery
P. O. Box 29012
Presidio of San Francisco
San Francisco, CA 94129
For information please contact: Golden Gate National Cemetery
(415) 761-1646

San Joaquin Valley National Cemetery
32053 West McCabe Road
Gustine, CA 95322
(209) 854-1040

CO
Fort Logan National Cemetery
3698 South Sheridan Boulevard
Denver, CO 80235
(303) 761-0117

Fort Lyon National Cemetery
VA Medical Center
Fort Lyon, CO 81038
For information please contact: Fort Logan National Cemetery
(303) 761-0117

FL
Barrancas National Cemetery
Naval Air Station
Pensacola, FL 32508-1099
(850) 452-3357 or 4196

Bay Pines National Cemetery
P. O. Box 477
Bay Pines, FL 33504-0477
For information please contact: Florida National Cemetery
(352) 793-7740

Florida National Cemetery
6502 SW 102nd Avenue
Bushnell, FL 33513
(352) 793-7740 or 1074

St. Augustine National Cemetery
104 Marine Street
St. Augustine, FL 32084
For information please contact: Florida National Cemetery
(352) 793-7740

GA
Marietta National Cemetery
500 Washington Avenue
Marietta, GA 30060
For information please contact: Chattanooga National Cemetery
(423) 855-6590

HI
National Memorial Cemetery of the Pacific
2177 Puowaina Drive
Honolulu, HI 96813-1729
(808) 566-1430

IL
Alton National Cemetery
600 Pearl Street
Alton, IL 62003
For information please contact: Jefferson Barracks National Cem.
(314) 260-8720

Camp Butler National Cemetery
5063 Camp Butler Road; RR #1
Springfield, IL 62707
(217) 492-4070

Danville National Cemetery
1900 East Main Street
Danville, IL 61832
(217) 431-6550

Mound City National Cemetery
P. O. Box 128
Mound City, IL 62963
For information please contact: Jefferson Barracks National Cem.
(314) 260-8720

Quincy National Cemetery
6th and Maine Street
Quncy, IL 62301
For information please contact: Rock Island National Cem. (309) 782-2094

Rock Island National Cemetery
P.O. Box 737
Moline, IL 61265
(309) 782-2094

IN
Crown Hill National Cemetery
700 West 38th Street
Indianapolis, IN 46208
For more information please contact: Marion National Cemetery
(765) 674-0284

Marion National Cemetery
VA Medical Center
Marion County
1700 East 38th Street
Marion, IN 46952
(765) 674-0284

New Albany National Cemetery
1943 Ekin Avenue
New Albany, IN 47150
For information please contact: Zachary Taylor National Cem.
(502) 893-3852

IA
Keokuk National Cemetery
1701 J Street
Keokuk, IA 52632
For information please contact: Rock Island National Cem.
(309) 782-2094

KS
Fort Leavenworth National Cemetery
Fort Leavenworth, KS 66027
For information please contact: Leavenworth National Cemetery
(913) 758-4105

Fort Scott National Cemetery
P. O. Box 917
Fort Scott, KS 66701
(316) 223-2840

Leavenworth National Cemetery
P. O. Box 1694
Leavenworth, KS 66048
(913) 758-4105

KY
Camp Nelson National Cemetery
6980 Danville Road
Nicholasville, KY 40356
(606) 885-5727

Cave Hill National Cemetery
701 Baxter Avenue
Louisville, KY 40204
For information please contact: Zachary Taylor National Cemetery
(502) 893-3852

Danville National Cemetery
277 North First Street
Danville, KY 40442
For information please contact: Camp Nelson National Cemetery
(606) 885-5727

Lebanon National Cemetery
20 Highway 208
Lebanon, KY 40033
(502) 692-3390

Lexington National Cemetery
833 West Main Street
Lexington, KY 40508
For information please contact: Camp Nelson National Cem.
(606) 885-5727

Mill Springs National Cemetery
Nancy, KY 42544
For information please contact: Camp Nelson National Cemetery
(606) 885-5727

Zachary Taylor National Cemetery
1701 Brownsboro Road
Louisville, KY 40207
(502) 893-3852

LA

Alexandria National Cemetery
209 East Shamrock Street
Pineville, LA 71360
For information please contact: Natchez National Cemetery
(601) 445-4981

Baton Rouge National Cemetery
220 North 19th Street
Baton Rouge, LA 70806
For information please contact: Port Hudson National Cemetery
(225) 654-3767

Port Hudson National Cemetery
20978 Port Hickey Road
Zachary, LA 70791
(225) 654-3767

ME

Togus National Cemetery
VA Medical and Regional Office Center
Togus, ME 04330
For information please contact: Massachusetts National Cemetery
(508) 563-7113

MD

Annapolis National Cemetery
800 West Street
Annapolis, MD 21401
For information please contact: Baltimore National Cemetery
(410) 644-9696

Baltimore National Cemetery
5501 Frederick Avenue
Baltimore, MD 21228
(410) 644-9696

Loudon Park National Cemetery
3445 Frederick Avenue
Baltimore, MD 21228
For information please contact: Baltimore National Cemetery
(410) 644-9696

MA
Massachusetts National Cemetery
Bourne, MA 02532
(508) 563-7113

MI
Fort Custer National Cemetery
15501 Dickman Road
Augusta, MI 49012
(616) 731-4164

MN
Fort Snelling National Cemetery
7601 34th Avenue South
Minneapolis, MN 55450-1199
(612) 726-1127

MS
Biloxi National Cemetery
P. O. Box 4968
Biloxi, MS 39535-4968
(228) 388-6668

Corinth National Cemetery
1551 Horton Street
Corinth, MS 38834
For information please contact: Memphis National Cemetery
(901) 386-8311

Natchez National Cemetery
41 Cemetery Road
Natchez, MS 39120
(601) 445-4981

MO
Jefferson Barracks National Cemetery
2900 Sheridan Road
St. Louis, MO 63125
(314) 260-8720

Jefferson City National Cemetery
1024 East McCarty Street
Jefferson City, MO 65101
For information please contact: Jefferson Barracks National Cem.
(314) 260-8720

Springfield National Cemetery
1702 East Seminole Street
Springfield, MO 65804
(417) 881-9499

NC
New Bern National Cemetery
1711 National Avenue
New Bern, NC 28560
(252) 637-2912

Raleigh National Cemetery
501 Rock Quarry Road
Raleigh, NC 27610
For information please contact: Salisbury National Cemetery
(704) 636-2661

Salisbury National Cemetery
202 Government Road
Salisbury, NC 28144
(704) 636-2661

Wilmington National Cemetery
2011 Market Street
Wilmington, NC 28403
For information please contact: New Bern National Cemetery
(252) 637-2912

NE
Fort McPherson National Cemetery
HCO1, Box 67
Maxwell, NE 69151
(308) 582-4433

NJ
Beverly National Cemetery
R.D. #1
Bridgeboro Road
Beverly, NJ 08010
(609) 877-5460

Finn's Point National Cemetery
RFD # 3, Fort Mott Road, Box 542
Salem, NJ 08079
For information please contact: Beverly National Cemetery
(609) 877-5460

NM
Fort Bayard National Cemetery
P. O. Box 189
Fort Bayard, NM 88036
For information please contact: Fort Bliss National Cemetery
(915) 564-0201

Santa Fe National Cemetery
501 North Guadalupe Street
Santa Fe, NM 87501
(505) 988-6400

NY
Bath National Cemetery
VA Medical Center
Bath, NY 14810
(607) 776-5480, Ext. 1293

Calverton National Cemetery
210 Princeton Boulevard
Calverton, NY 11933-1031
(516) 727-5410 or 5770

Cypress Hills National Cemetery
625 Jamaica Avenue
Brooklyn, NY 11208
For information please contact: Long Island National Cemetery
(516) 454-4949

Long Island National Cemetery
2040 Wellwood Avenue
Farmingdale, NY 11735-1211
(516) 454-4949

Woodlawn National Cemetery
1825 Davis Street
Elmira, NY 14901
For information please contact: Bath National Cemetery
(607) 776-5480, Ext. 1293

OH
Dayton National Cemetery
VA Medical Center
4100 West Third Street
Dayton, OH 45428-1008
(937) 262-2115

OK
Fort Gibson National Cemetery
1423 Cemetery Road
Fort Gibson, OK 74434
(918) 478-2334

OR
Eagle Point National Cemetery
2763 Riley Road
Eagle Point, OR 97524
(541) 826-2511

Roseburg National Cemetery
VA Medical Center
Roseburg, OR 97470
For information please contact: Willamette National Cemetery
(503) 273-5250

Willamette National Cemetery
11800 S.E. Mt. Scott Boulevard
Portland, OR 97266-6937
(503) 273-5250

PA
Indiantown Gap National Cemetery
R. R. #2, P. O. Box 484
Annville, PA 17003-9618
(717) 865-5254

Philadelphia National Cemetery
Haines Street and Limekiln Pike
Philadelphia, PA 19138
For information please contact: Beverly National Cemetery
(609) 877-5460

PR
Puerto Rico National Cemetery
P. O. Box 1298
Bayamon, PR 00960
(787) 798-6720

SC
Beaufort National Cemetery
1601 Boundary Street
Beaufort, SC 29902
(803) 524-3925

Florence National Cemetery
803 East National Cemetery Road
Florence, SC 29501
(803) 669-8783

SD
Black Hills National Cemetery
P. O. Box 640
Sturgis, SD 57785
(605) 347-3830 or 7299

Fort Meade National Cemetery
Old Stone Road
Sturgis, SD 57785
For information please contact: Black Hills National Cemetery
(605) 347-3830 or 7299

Hot Springs National Cemetery
VA Medical Center
Hot Springs, SD 57747
For information please contact: Black Hills National Cemetery
(605) 347-3830 or 7299

TN
Chattanooga National Cemetery
1200 Bailey Avenue
Chattanooga, TN 37404
(423) 855-6590

Knoxville National Cemetery
939 Tyson Street, N.W.
Knoxville, TN 37917
For information please contact: Mountain Home National Cem.
(423) 461-7935

Memphis National Cemetery
3568 Townes Avenue
Memphis, TN 38122
(901) 386-8311

Mountain Home National Cemetery
P. O. Box 8
Mountain Home, TN 37684
(423) 461-7935

Nashville National Cemetery
1420 Gallatin Road South
Madison, TN 37115-4619
(615) 736-2839

TX
Fort Bliss National Cemetery
5200 Fred Wilson Road
P. O. Box 6342
Fort Bliss, TX 79906
(915) 564-0201

Fort Sam Houston National Cemetery
1520 Harry Wurzbach Road
San Antonio, TX 78209
(210) 820-3891

Houston National Cemetery
10410 Veterans Memorial Drive
Houston, TX 77038
(281) 447-8686

Kerrville National Cemetery
VA Medical Center
3600 Memorial Boulevard
Kerrville, TX 78028
For information please contact: Fort Sam Houston National Cem.
(210) 820-3891

San Antonio National Cemetery
517 Paso Hondo Street
San Antonio, TX 78202
For information please contact: Fort Sam Houston National Cem.
(210) 820-3891

VA
Alexandria National Cemetery
1450 Wilkes Street
Alexandria, VA 22314
For information please contact: Culpeper National Cemetery
(540) 825-0027

Balls Bluff National Cemetery
Route 7
Leesburg, VA 22075
For information please contact: Culpeper National Cemetery
(540) 825-0027

City Point National Cemetery
10th Avenue and Davis Street
Hopewell, VA 23860
For information please contact: Fort Harrison National Cemetery
(804) 795-2031

Cold Harbor National Cemetery
Route 156 North
Mechanicsville, VA 23111
For information please contact: Fort Harrison National Cemetery
(804) 795-2031

Culpeper National Cemetery
305 U.S. Avenue
Culpeper, VA 22701
(540) 825-0027

Danville National Cemetery
721 Lee Street
Danville, VA 24541
For information please contact: Salisbury National Cemetery
(704) 636-2661

Fort Harrison National Cemetery
8620 Varina Road
Richmond, VA 23231
(804) 795-2031

Glendale National Cemetery
8301 Willis Church Road
Richmond, VA 23231
For information please contact: Fort Harrison National Cemetery
(804) 795-2031

Hampton National Cemetery
Cemetery Road at Marshall Avenue
Hampton, VA 23667
(757) 723-7104

Hampton National Cemetery
VA Medical Center
Emancipation Drive
Hampton, VA 23667
(757) 723-7104

Quantico National Cemetery
P. O. Box 10
18424 Joplin Road (Route 619)
Triangle, VA 22172
(703) 690-2217 (metro) (703) 221-2183 (local)

Richmond National Cemetery
1701 Williamsburg Road
Richmond, VA 23231
For information please contact: Fort Harrison National Cemetery
(804) 795-2031

Seven Pines National Cemetery
400 East Williamsburg Road
Sandston, VA 23150
For information please contact: Fort Harrison National Cemetery
(804) 795-2031

Staunton National Cemetery
901 Richmond Avenue
Staunton, VA 24401
For information please contact: Culpeper National Cemetery
(540) 825-0027

Winchester National Cemetery
401 National Avenue
Winchester, VA 22601
For information please contact: Culpeper National Cemetery
(540) 825-0027

WA
Tahoma National Cemetery
18600 Southeast 240th Street
Kent, WA 98042-4868
(425) 413-9614

WV
Grafton National Cemetery
431 Walnut Street
Grafton, WV 26354
For information please contact: West Virginia National Cem.
(304) 265-2044

West Virginia National Cemetery
Route 2, Box 127
Grafton, WV 26354
(304) 265-2044

WI
Wood National Cemetery
5000 West National Avenue
Building 1301
Milwaukee, WI 53295-4000
(414) 382-5300

INDEX

advance directive, 36
assets, 24
beneficiaries, 24
brain death, 53
cardiac death, 53
cash value, 29
cemetery, 82
Certificates of Deposit, 19
changes in ownership and title, 20
columbarium, 85
cremains, 85
cremation, 74
crypts, 84
death of a pet, 103
durable power of attorney, 37
estate, 24
executor, 24
expedited probate, 26
grantor, 26
group life, 28
healthcare declaration, 36
healthcare power of attorney, 39
healthcare proxy, 38
hospice, 41
income taxes, Federal and State, 20
intestate, 25
jointly held bank accounts, 25
jointly owned property, 20

jointly incurred debt, 20
joint tenants, 26
living will, 36
loss of a child, 95
loss of a spouse, 91
mausoleums, 84
markers, 84
memorial societies, 69
monuments, 84
national cemeteries, 85
non-probate property, 25
ordinary life, 29
Patient Self-Determination Act, 37
policies, 29
pour-over will, 27
permanently unconscious, 40
pre-arrangement, 64
pre-payment, 64
pre-need planning, 65
premium, 29
probate, 25
probate property, 25
revocable living trust, 26
safe deposit box, 19
settlor, 26
Social Security, 31
successor trustee, 27
tenants in common, 25
term life, 29
terminally ill, 40
trustee, 26
universal life, 29
viatical settlements, 30
viator, 31
will, 24

Send *You Can't Leave Till You Do the Paperwork: Matters of Life and Death* to a friend or loved one by calling 888-7XLIBRIS

Hardback....... $25   Paperback....... $14.40

Shipping and Handling....... $4.95 (first book), $1 each additional book

Check or Money Order   Visa   Mastercard   American Express

Xlibris Corporation
888-7XLIBRIS   215-923-4686   Fax 215-923-4685